I MATTER

Finding Meaning in Your Life at Any Age

Harlan Rector and Edward Mickolus
VOLUME ONE

Cross & Partners
Ponte Vedra, Florida

I MATTER:
Finding Meaning in Your Life at Any Age

Harlan Rector and Edward F. Mickolus

First Edition October 2020

ISBN-978-1-7350747-1-9

Published in the United States by Cross and Partners II, LLC

Book Design, Cover and Typesetting by
Cynthia J. Kwitchoff (CJKCREATIVE.COM)

TABLE OF CONTENTS

Editors' Introduction

After Harlan wrote his first book, *Once Upon a Corner in Detroit*, a collection of profiles and caricatures of celebrities who were interviewed at WJR Radio in the early 1970s, Ed egged him on with the question, "It's a promising start. So what's your next book?" Harlan mulled this over for a while, and prayed on it. He soon received an answer: the idea for this book, a look at how people find purpose in life at any age and stage of life. How can life, ultimately, Matter? When looking back and forward on one's life, did I mean something? What was my purpose?

Viktor Frankel viewed adult development as *Man's Search for Meaning*. Gail Sheehy organized that search chronologically, calling them *Passages*. Daniel Levinson's more formal building upon Sheehy's work deemed them *Seasons of a Man's Life* and *Seasons of a Woman's Life*. We've combined these concepts, asking our authors to talk about points in their lives in which someone or some development dramatically affected their lives, preferably for the better, or they affected someone's life, again, preferably for the better. Our chapters look at all points of one's life, from childhood up through death.

Seized with the idea that we had not cornered the market on wisdom in this area, we reached out to our colleagues, some of whom we know quite well, some known only by reputation. Their replies were heartening; many inspiring.

Our authors come from all walks of life, and mirror the diversity of the American experience. They represent different races, genders, sexual orientations, ages, socioeconomic status, religious preferences, ethnic heritage, and professions. They come from the worlds of sports, entertainment, business, government, espionage, education, social work, and emergency medicine. Some seek meaning in their faith; others in their works; still others in their immediate family, extended family, or family trees.

We hope you enjoy reading this book as much as we have compiling—and in some cases, writing—it. We encourage you to share in the writing part. At the end of each chapter, we've left blank space for you to write your micro-memoir of how you found meaning at each stage of your life. Do something kind each day and make a note of it.

We're planning to put together a Volume II of this book. If you'd like to participate, please send your submissions to us at hrector234@ aol.com and edmickolus@gmail.com.

Thanks for reading this book and for making a difference by your lives.

Harlan and Ed
Somewhere in Northeast Florida
2020

I MATTER

CHAPTER 1

The Age of Innocence: Childhood / Elementary School

ℰᴏᴄℛ

Christmas 1947
By Sue Jones

I was four years old; we lived in a one-bedroom apartment in Chicago. I shared the bedroom with my Grandma and brother. My parents slept in the in-a-door bed in the living room. There was a couch in the dining room for visiting relatives.

Christmas was in the air. I had a brand-new wool snow suit—bright green with red trim—perfect for the season. Outside I watched snow flakes melt on my jacket and felt them disappear when I stuck out my tongue.

Santa would be coming soon. We went to see one of his helpers. The real Santa was busy at the North Pole. I didn't give the fill-in Santa a Christmas list. Santa always knew exactly the right present for me.

I rarely played with my dolls, but tradition required my dolls be set out at night a few weeks before Christmas; Santa's elves collected them and took them to the North Pole to the doll hospital. They were examined, treated and fitted with new outfits. I dutifully left them one night, but when I woke in the morning they were still there. My mother said the elves only stop when little girls have been very, very good. I was always good, so I am not sure what mistake occurred, but the next night they were gone.

Every afternoon I listened to a special radio show called the Cinnamon Bear. I loved it. We had a leather-bound book embossed with a wreath and candle called the *Christmas Messenger*. I still bring it out at Christmas. Grandma read me the stories and poems and I looked at the magical pictures. My favorite was The Sugar Plum Tree. There was a very sad story about a little "orfant" boy named Billy Peebles. He found a new home and had a real Christmas, so it ended happily.

Forty children lived in our apartment building. One starry night we congregated in the courtyard. Santa was on the rooftop with his sack. Somehow he got down to the ground. None of us had fireplaces, but there was a big boiler in the basement. His suit was clean, so I don't think he slid down there. He gave each of us a preview present—a game with little silver balls. There were holes in the picture where the balls fit if you tilted it just right. I could never get the balls in their slots, but I loved the picture — it was Rudolph — a very special reindeer who helped Santa.

Sue at age 4

A week before Christmas Dad carried in the Christmas tree. It was tall and straight and had short needles. We decorated it with large multi-colored lights. We spent a long time carefully placing the tinsel on the branches strand by strand — throwing was forbidden. I don't know how the tree fit in the living room along with the desk, sofa, chairs, and bookcase. There had to be room for the bed to come down at night for Mom and Dad.

With only the lights from the tree I watched and listened. I saw the lights dance on the ceiling and heard the needles falling from the tree. There were few needles left by Christmas, and the tree was taken down shortly after the big day.

Santa arrived — no problem about the lack of fireplace. The dolls were back looking very pretty. My sock was bulging with nuts, a candy cane, an orange and apple, lifesavers, and a comic book. My perfect presents that year were a pair of red boots and a clear plastic umbrella printed with pictures of traffic lights. I was starting kindergarten in January; I would wear my boots and carry the umbrella on rainy days. I couldn't wait.

1947 was a wonderful year.

⚮

The Cherry Tree
By Sue Jones

My parents, brother, Grandma, and I moved from our one-bedroom apartment to a large old home. Two ladies lived next door — Mrs. Kitzelman and her companion, Miss Zaletel — names reflective of the wonderful Chicago melting pot. I knew how to say their names, but they asked me to call them Mrs. K and Miss Z.

They invited me to lunch in their beautiful sun porch; they served delicious soup, biscuits with cherry preserves and tea from delicate flowered china. My brother was not included; it was not a place for boys. My parents weren't asked, either.

It was the perfect place for an eight-year-old girl. I talked with their bird, and admired their beautiful yard and magnificent cherry tree. The tree was in full bloom and Mrs. K and Miss Z said they hoped when the cherries were ripe I would help pick them before the birds ate them all.

One night I was awakened by howling wind, driving rain, and an ear-shattering boom. The roof was still overhead, but I knew something had happened. In the morning I looked out the window and the cherry tree had crashed to the ground—ripe cherries glistening on the branches.

We went to work and stripped the tree. Miss Z made jelly, preserves and fancy tarts. Grandma took out her huge baking pan. It must have been larger than 9 by 13. We pitted cherries; she deftly rolled out dough and created the magnificent pan of cherry slices—topped with a thin glaze of frosting. They looked just like the cherry slices sold in the neighborhood bakery, but they were so much better.

Fourth of July brought hamburgers, hot dogs, corn on the cob, baked beans, marshmallows toasted on a stick and cherry slices. I should have been sad the cherry tree was gone, but we had 14 apple trees in our yard, and Grandma made great apple cobbler, too.

Sue Jones is a retired special education teacher. She has been married for 54 years and has two sons. She lived in Illinois for many years, then in southern Florida before moving to Ponte Vedra, Florida. She loves walking the beach and hiking the beautiful Florida nature trails. She enjoys reading all genres and writing stories and poems.

ℰℭ

The Cave-In
By Carol Pierskalla

It is the summer of 1940. I am four and a half years old. Two neighborhood boys and I are playing "Lost at Sea" in a huge tractor tire inner tube on the front lawn of our house in Minneapolis, Minnesota. Suddenly the ground opens up and swallows us. I am sucked down into cool dirt.

My mother was hanging clothes on the lines in the back yard when she noticed a change in the excited screams from the front yard. "Lost at Sea" had ceased to be a game and the screams took on a realistic urgency. Rushing to the front yard she was confronted by a huge gaping hole in the center of the lawn. Horrified, she peered over the edge of the hole. Two small, terrified faces looked up at her.

"Where is Carol Ann?" she asked.

They both pointed down. "Down there," they said.

"Hang on! I'll be back in a minute!" And then she was gone.

She ran next door to the Roses' house. She knew that Mr. Rose was a fireman who worked the night shift so he slept during the day. She told a startled Mrs. Rose, "The children are buried in the dirt! Tell Mr. Rose to come right away!" She ran to the garage where she took a ladder off the garage wall. Half dragging it and half carrying it, she ran to the front where Mr. Rose, in his pajamas, was now lying on the ground talking quietly to the two boys.

"She's buried down there, Annie," he told my mother. "My wife is calling the fire department but we can't wait. You'll have to help me get down there."

They lowered the ladder over the crumbling edges of the hole, propping it up near the bottom on a small pipe. They were fearful that the pipe could burst, flooding the hole, yet more afraid that setting the ladder down on the dirt could accidentally hurt me. Mr. Rose lowered himself into the hole. He began digging around the boys with his bare hands. "I've found her face…I'm uncovering her nose and mouth and trying to clean them out."

And then the blessed words, "She's breathing!"

My nose is full of dirt. My eyes are full of dirt. My ears are full of dirt. But I am out of the hole. Everyone, the neighbors, the police, the newspaper people, clap their hands for me. I am okay.

Mother asks me if I called for her when I was down there in the dirt.

I look at her in puzzled wonder. "No," I said, "I called for God."

Carol Spargo Pierskalla, Ph.D. has been a teacher, dean of students and consultant. She was also the National Director of Older Adult Ministries for American Baptist Churches, USA. In the years before her retirement she traveled all over the US, including Alaska and Puerto Rico, teaching, doing workshops and preaching on how to care for the older adults in our communities and churches.

&CR

Finding What Matters
By Carl Hermann

I really liked kindergarten except on days when the sky turned gray. If there was thunder and lightning I would leave my table, leave school, and walk home.

Of course, the school did not approve of this and neither did my mother. Each time it happened I would be marched back to school, sometimes under an umbrella. I finally decided leaving was not worth the trouble.

Kindergarten and the first couple of grades were a golden time. The teachers liked me, my grades were good, I could select activities for the class, I was able to choose the position I played in softball, I won foot races, and my marble collection grew when we played marbles for keeps. Life was good.

Then mid-semester of our second year, two new boys came into our class. Both were named Bill. I'm using their real last names because they seem appropriate. Bill Belt was short but husky and had a tendency to question how things were being done. Bill Topp was a half a head taller than me and he felt he should have his opinions respected.

We became friends but I knew my reign was over. That time, I guess, it didn't matter as much as I thought.

When I was nine years old, my family moved from Webster Groves, a St. Louis suburb, into St Louis City. I was enrolled into the fourth grade at Kennard School.

Kennard was one of the city schools designed by the nationally-known St. Louis architect William B. Ittner. The façade of the building had handsome architectural details and the third-floor music room had stained glass windows. The halls and the playground were kept in pristine condition under the watchful eye of the principal, Miss Beulah Baker. No student used the front door and we were lined up and marched into and out of the rear of the building.

It was a real neighborhood school. Everyone walked to school and walked home and back for lunch. In the several blocks around our house there was a great variety in the way fathers, at that time, made a living. There was a doctor, mailman, dentist, insurance salesman, streetcar conductor, minister, and lawyer. One of the goals of public schools was to bring students from different backgrounds together. It was being met at that time at Kennard Public School. The teachers, all career women, did try to make each student feel that they mattered and I know I felt well-trained to enter high school.

During summer vacations my mother took my brother and me to weekly programs at the St. Louis Art Museum that involved games, drawing, and lectures — and I was hooked on art.

Carl L. Hermann was born in 1925 in St. Louis, Missouri. After elementary school, and fully prepared for higher learning, he graduated from Southwest High School. On to The Washington University School of Fine Arts, where his graduation was temporarily postponed by his three years of service in the U.S. Navy during WWII. Carl's career in art began in several advertising agencies and commercial art studios. Then, after thirty-two years with Maritz, Inc., the sales promotion, travel and communication conglomerate, Carl retired. He didn't hang up his brushes, though. He joined other artists at the St. Louis Artist Guild every week to enjoy their company and the pleasure of painting together. He still paints.

ℰℛ

Making Lemonade
By Harlan Rector

There was no such thing as a babysitter when I was growing up. My mom and dad took my older brother and me with them everywhere they went. My earliest recollections begin when I was four years old and my grandfather died. My brother and I, of course, went with our mom and dad to the funeral home and I made the most of the situation by standing at the front door and saying to whomever came in, "Are you here to see my Grandpa? He's in Parlor A." My mother told me about this later. I was too young to understand the old adage "When you're given a lemon, make lemonade", but I used it throughout my life.

When I was four months old, my Protestant family moved to south St. Louis, from a mid-city location, smack dab in the middle of a huge Roman Catholic parish. Lots of friends to play with on weekends, but after school the parish kids were busy with church/school activities so I was handed another lemon.

On some of our trips, our parents took us to visit my mother's kindergarten friend on the outskirts of St. Louis. The family, with two children much older than my brother and me, lived behind the grocery store they owned. Their son, Stanley, was an amateur magician and would perform every time we visited. I was hooked. Magic became my lemonade. One Christmas my brother gave me a $10 set of magic tricks, worth $100 in today's economy. I practiced in front of a mirror every weekday after school and sometimes on Saturday if it was raining. When I was a pre-teen, and I managed to save $5, I'd take a bus and streetcar up to north St. Louis and spend an entire Saturday at Don Lawton's Magic Den. In

wonder I watched local magicians come into the store to see demonstrations of new tricks up Don Lawton's sleeve. They talked and laughed and traded magic secrets with other magicians. It was like a party that I was crashing, only they didn't pay a bit of attention to me. By Saturday afternoon I would get up the courage to spend my $5 and head home. I became moderately adept at my tricks and gave performances to scout troops, birthday parties and anyone who asked. I'm not sure I was ever paid for doing my prestidigitation, but the applause was enough.

Along the way I traded my magic for piano lessons. Much later when my wife gave birth to our unexpected identical twin boys, I considered taking up magic again because I had a built-in magic act finale, a disappearing/reappearing boy trick that would bring down the house.

My wife wisely burst that lemonade balloon and put an end to a career of magic. The allure of magic surfaced several times later in life and so did making lemonade, which you can read about in Chapter 4.

Harlan Rector Bio

It only takes a few misplaced letters to change fearless to foolish. Happily, in my case I was more often the former. In second grade, when asked by the teacher what we wanted to be when we grew up, most boys chose cowboy or soldier. I didn't think any cowboys came from St. Louis, Missouri and Pearl Harbor happened just a few months before and soldiering wasn't glamorous yet, so I fearlessly said, "I want to be an artist."

When I was given the inspiration for this book's title and the rough idea of its contents, I shared it with Ed Mickolus. He immediately suggested the sub-title, "Finding meaning in your life at any age." That gave our book the direction it needed. The rest was easy, getting other writers to fill the pages with their own positive stories. My intention was not to be foolishly verbose but once I started thinking about contributing to one chapter, it led to another and another and now my bio is in chapters 1, 3, 4, 5 and 6.

Creative people, generally, are their own worst critic and walk a thin line between applause and being ignored. With that in mind, there are two things

I am most proud of in my careers and in my life. Two awards for television and radio production and my family. Creative on their own, my wife and five children have supported my fearlessness and overlooked my foolishness.

I thank God for His inspiration and pray that every reader will find meaning in their life.

ℂ℁ℂ

A Love Letter
By Pat Krause

Dear Popi,

It's been almost 11 years since you've been gone and I still miss you! I have such sweet memories of you from my growing-up years in Elmhurst. Some of my happiest childhood reminiscences revolve around time spent with you. You had a way of bringing smiles to my heart and to my face. You still do!!

Do you remember how Linda and I would rush up to the 90th Street subway station to meet you as you came off the train? Sometimes we would jump up into your arms and nearly knock you over! But you always seemed so delighted to see "your girls"! We would be full of news of our day and anxious for you to find the "mail" we left for you in your dresser drawer, tucked in between your neatly pressed handkerchiefs or underneath your socks…always with lots of OOO's and XXX's included in those little love notes.

Remember how we used to braid your graying hair and then put ribbons in it and make you pose for pictures? How did you have the patience to put up with all of that? And the bedtime routines… the litany of "nighty nightgowns, pajamas-pajamas, and sleepy tight"… all followed by your tucking us cozily into our twin beds. Only this ritual, faithfully performed, could send us off into dreamland each night.

Sometimes I feel so close to you, Popi. Did you hear me last week out on the golf course as I stood over the ball, begging your intercession for a good shot? Do you hear me when I complain and ask your help when I am overwhelmed when things are not going well with Mom? Do you see her struggles? Do you know how much she longs to be with you?

Do you see me in the garden picking tomatoes? I remember how you loved tomatoes and would eat them for lunch on a slice of bread with lots of salt. You put salt on everything, even watermelon! A few of your grandchildren have picked up on that habit!

Do you see me when I am at prayer with Snowy on my lap? I bet you agree that she is the most beautiful cat in the world. You were so faithful to your prayer. I can still see you kneeling at the foot of your bed in your sleeveless undershirt saying the Hail Mary and Our Father in French. That picture is firmly implanted in my memory. Nothing got in the way of your prayer time. We knew not to disturb you then.

Popi, you always made me feel loved…and special. I thank you for that and for all you taught me about life—to believe in myself and to cherish all the little things that make each day worthwhile. Our spiritual bond is very strong and I hope that someday we'll be able to enjoy the heavenly realms together and maybe play golf together on a beautiful celestial golf course in the clouds.

—*Your Loving Daughter*

Pat Krause lives with her husband of 50+ years in Ponte Vedra, Florida. She is a member of the Del Webb Writer's Club and has been published in the club anthology, Riverwood Writes. An avid writer, photographer and poet, Pat's faith, love of nature and personal relationships inspire her writing.

∞∞

Thank You, Chuck
By Greg Barry

Sometimes we're beneficiaries of sudden good fortune such as winning the lottery or being uninjured after a serious car crash. Other times we're beneficiaries of good fortune which is earned, such as studying hard for a final exam then acing it or going the extra mile on a work project and being rewarded for it.

But this isn't about that. This is about being the beneficiary of something more gradual and it isn't quantifiable. It's about learning valuable life lessons in an unexpected way from an unexpected source.

My father was a good man; a very good man. He was honest, hard-working, steady, careful, deliberate, reliable, dependable and frugal. He was the son of Irish immigrants. He was also a child of the Depression era and those feelings always stayed with him. He provided for us and he loved my mother and his children.

Family friends lived up the street from us. My father worked at the same organization as Chuck, my good friend Tom's father. Chuck was about eight years younger than my father for whom he had great respect. Our families shared a lot of memories over the years including going to ballgames, celebrating holidays and occasionally vacationing together.

Chuck was our coach in community sports leagues, including baseball, football and basketball. He always drove Tom and me and a bunch of other teammates to practices and games. He would stop at 7-Eleven after practices and buy us all sodas even if was close to dinner time. He liked to laugh and joke around with us.

Chuck taught me about how to enjoy life. It wasn't anything he shared with me directly. I learned from observing him. He was a successful businessman but every so often, if there was something particularly interesting to do, he would play hooky from work. He'd take Tom and me to a Washington Senators baseball game or maybe to watch Washington's football team on their first day of practice.

He taught me about the lighter side of life. He was all about working hard and playing hard. He had many interests and a biting, sarcastic sense of humor. He could also be self-deprecating which made him seem more human and a little less parental.

Over the years, I hadn't thought much about Chuck's influence over me and how I would adopt some of his personality traits. But a few years ago I read a journal article about child development. The theory is that at about the age of 12, children, especially boys, often subconsciously seek out a mentor to fill in developmental gaps and help to develop tools and strategies for handling life's many confounding situations.

In my life BC (before Chuck), I lacked an ability to express myself the way I wanted to, I wouldn't take risks, I couldn't communicate well with adults, I embarrassed easily and I had difficulty accepting criticism or praise.

Through my observations of Chuck, starting at about the age of 12, emulating how he handled situations, some of my struggles became less paralyzing. It didn't happen suddenly, but over time I felt more confident and better able to manage issues and problems more effectively. The life lessons I learned from Chuck during that time still serve me to this day. While I'm not naïve enough to believe it was all about Chuck, much of it was.

I've never spoken with my friend Tom about how, through osmosis, I adopted many of his father's life management skills but someday I will. I now think about Chuck often and even though he doesn't know how much he was able to positively influence me, I'll always know what he did for me in so many ways and I feel forever indebted to him for it.

Greg Barry grew up in Fairfax, Virginia. He was an emergency medical technician for six years at Santa Monica Hospital near Los Angeles. Greg earned undergraduate and graduate degrees in health administration while living in California. He met his wife Laura while working at UCLA Medical Center. Greg and Laura spent 20 years living in the Twin Cities working in the health care field. They now live in northeastern Florida.

As a classic film enthusiast, Greg hosts monthly classic film screenings for the nearly 300 members of his community's Classic Films Group. Some of his other interests include literature, post-1950s contemporary music and sports, particularly baseball and tennis. Greg enjoys playing softball, tennis and beach Frisbee.

Greg has joined a talented group of actors from his community as a part-time member of the simulated patient program at Jacksonville University. He works primarily with graduate students in the speech therapy, nursing and psychology departments.

Greg contributed 11 biographies for sketch artist Harlan Rector's Once Upon a Corner in Detroit. He contributed four humorous essays to an anthology of essays, poems and reflections in Riverwood Writes, published in 2019. He also contributes to a monthly newsletter for a hospice facility in Jacksonville, Florida.

&)C&

Having, and Perhaps Becoming, That Special Teacher: Influencing Lives for Decades

By Ed Mickolus

Many of us still remember that first great teacher (and maybe it was your first-grade teacher!) who inspired us into a lifelong love of learning (and, apparently, alliteration!).

For me it was my 5th grade teacher, Robert Strom, who we were told was working on his Harvard Ph.D. while keeping himself financially afloat by teaching. You don't find many Ph.D.s in elementary school classrooms, but why not? In addition to the standard things on the required learning objectives for 5th graders (and don't you wish you can remember some of them while watching *Are You Smarter Than a 5th Grader?*), I vividly remember his lessons on, of all things, centuries-old operas, which I'm pretty sure wasn't on the annual Michigan standardized tests. He merrily walked us through the music, the librettos, the costumes, the history of the period, the biographies of the composers and conductors, you name it. Puccini, Verdi, Monteverdi, Mozart, Rossini, Wagner, Purcell, Handel, Berlioz, Tchaikovsky, Dvorak, and Debussy were as eagerly discussed by us as the exploits of Mantle, Maris, Kaline, Aaron, and Mays. He hosted fast-paced oral quizzes on opera, in the style of a game show, and constantly showered us with praise.

Dr. Strom's operatic overtures came in handy when I was on an episode of Detroit's High School Bowl television competition (an early precursor to College Bowl, Jeopardy, and trivia games held at bars and civic associations) and the category was Opera! We set a record for the biggest margin of loss overall, but we ran the table on the opera questions.

Looking back on his enthusiastic and inspirational teaching style, I later was attracted to trying to become That teacher for someone and have developed a love for teaching, mentoring, and coaching. I've coached national Model United Nations championship teams at the high school and college level; taught at various universities, graduate schools, and federal training facilities; serve as a roleplayer for nursing, counseling, and speech therapy students; and now teach in an adult education program affiliated with the Osher Lifelong Learning Institute. On occasion, I still get an email or LinkedIn note from my course alums, following up on how some offhand comment made a positive difference in their lives.

And I still play trivia.

Dr. Strom made a difference that echoed through decades of my life. I hope I've done the same for at least some of my students.

Dr. Edward Mickolus, after graduating from Georgetown University, wrote the first doctoral dissertation on international terrorism while earning an M.A., M.Phil., and Ph.D. from Yale University. He then served in analytical, operational, management, and staff positions in the Central Intelligence Agency for 33 years, where he was CIA's first full-time analyst on international terrorism; analyzed African political, economic, social, military, and leadership issues; wrote political-psychological assessments of world leaders; and managed collection, counterintelligence, and covert action programs against terrorists, drug traffickers, weapons proliferators, and hostile espionage services.

He founded Vinyard Software, Inc., whose products include ITERATE (International Terrorism: Attributes of Terrorist Events) text and numeric datasets and DOTS (Data on Terrorist Suspects). Clients include 200 universities in two dozen countries.

His 41 books include a series of multi-volume chronologies and biographies on international terrorism; 31 book chapters; 100 articles and reviews in refereed scholarly journals and newspapers and presentations to professional societies; and 15 humorous publications.

For the following ten years, he was a senior instructor for SAIC and its spinoff, Leidos, Inc. He taught as the Deborah M. Hixon Professor of Intelligence Tradecraft and was a Board of Advisors member at the Daniel Morgan Graduate School in Washington, D.C. and teaches at the University of North Florida and Jacksonville University.

His books include America's Funniest Memes: Coronavirus Edition; Terrorism Worldwide 2019-2020 (a continuation of a 15-volume series); the seven-volume Terrorist List; Spycraft for Thriller Writers; More Stories from Langley: Another Glimpse Inside the CIA; His Words (a collection of every word said by Jesus in the Bible); The Counterintelligence Chronology; The 50 Worst Terrorist Attacks; Food with Thought: The Wit and Wisdom of Chinese Fortune Cookies; Coaching Winning Model United Nations Teams (with Tom Brannan); The Literature of Terrorism; Combatting International Terrorism: A Quantitative Analysis; Take My Weight, Please: Head-to-Toe Fitness for Seniors – the Cowboy Joe Way (with Joe Rendon); Briefing for the Boardroom and the Situation Room; Stories from Langley; The Secret Book of CIA Humor; The Secret Book of Intelligence Community Humor; and Two Spies Walk Into a Bar.

He is currently working on a series of intelligence thrillers and murder mysteries, including White Noise Whispers, co-authored with Tracy Tripp. He and his wife, Susan Schjelderup, dote on their daughter, Dr. Ciana Mickolus. Buy his books, or the terrorists win!

Notes for your memories of this age:

I MATTER

CHAPTER 2

The Age of Learning: High School / College

℘ℭ

A Tribute in Time
By Sally Wahl Constain

Miss Rosenblum was my Social Studies teacher in Long Island City High School between 1959 and 1962. If you looked at her closely, you would have seen a lovely lady. Auburn waves framed a creamy complexion, highlighted by rouge-tinted cheeks. But there was very little chance for a close look. She sat in the back of the classroom, hidden behind the *New York Telegram* each afternoon, as we, the students, copied and answered questions from the blackboard. Many thought of her as burnt out.

But there is always a backstory. What was hers? A lost love, a thwarted career? I cannot thank her for inspirational history lessons, but I do owe her a lot of gratitude for one important contribution to my high school years. Student Court! Miss Helen Rosenblum was the faculty advisor for this wonderful elective. I think she might have designed the protocol. She did a great job. (Maybe she had wanted to study law, but was discouraged because she was a girl. I was.)

For three delightful years, eighth period was spent in her classroom with other members of the court, trying fellow students for such infractions as tardiness, smoking in the bathroom or skipping study hall. We had scripts to follow, and rotated taking the parts of defense attorney, prosecutor, judge and jury. Punishments usually were warnings or after-school detention. We were professional and just, and I loved every minute of it. Once Miss Rosenblum had taught us what to do, she retreated to her back-of-the-room seat, but was there if needed. We were a tight-knit group, enjoying our times together, and I even have a high school letter with the scales of justice on it.

At our fiftieth high school reunion at Ricardo's Catering Hall, right in front of Astoria Park, my friend, Phoebe, thanked me for having encouraged her to join Student Court. I said that it was so much fun, but how come none of us ever got beaten up for our efforts? Phoebe, never missing a beat, told me it was because we were fair. Very true, so thanks again, Miss Rosenblum. You taught us well.

Sally Wahl Constain is a lifelong lover of stories. She was an elementary school teacher and librarian in New York City for more than thirty years. She was president of the Writers Group at Del Webb, Ponte Vedra, Florida for the past three years. She is the author of The Keys to Fanny, a work of historical fiction. Her poetry chapbook, Sometimes I Wonder, collects twelve inspiring poems on our common human experience. Her latest book, Random Reflections, is an anthology of essays and poems, some based on family stories. She is presently writing poetry when inspired by emotions and circumstances, and is working on a sequel to The Keys to Fanny.

ℰℭ

Once Upon a Life in Three Words
By George McGovern

"**Typical**" would describe what I was, "**average**" would describe how I was, and "**follower**" would describe where I was in relation to my peers.

I was a typical kid growing up in New Jersey. I was the oldest son, second child of seven, in a home that gave only token attention to church but embraced the values of family, honesty, hard work, and respect for authority. I was **typical**. I teased my siblings, loved McDonald's hamburgers, watched a lot of TV, played sports, wanted to be part of an "in" crowd, and tried to get away with as much as I could. I was **typical**.

I was also **average**. I made average grades in school, was an average athlete, and was average looking. I was part of an average family that lived in an average house in an average neighborhood and went on average vacations.

I never made much of an impression no matter what setting I was in. For example, I can remember my 10th grade English teacher writing a poem about the class. The poem consisted of a unique attribute of each student in his class. I was the only one he forgot to include in the poem. However, going unnoticed had its benefits. There was a time in high school when a friend and I skipped out on a class and the teacher only observed that my friend was missing.

Part of the issue in my being **average** was that I never set any goals. I gravitated to taking life as it came rather than shaping my life as I went. I bounced from one sport to another and this, combined with my **average** athletic abilities, resulted in a lack of proficiency in any. The only goal I can remember setting in high school was to win the "most popular guy" award for the senior class. I worked hard at being everybody's friend, and it was a big disappointment when I found out I didn't get it. I was **average**.

So I was **typical** and **average** and also a **follower**. When I was in high school, I hung around with a bunch of guys; we called ourselves the "gusto guys". We drank a lot of beer, organized or attended all the high school parties, and tried to live out our motto which was "I don't care." I was not one of the leaders of the gusto guys. I didn't come up with the motto. I didn't organize the parties or excursions. I joined in the activities. I followed the directions that were set by the pacesetters.

Living as a **typical, average follower** persisted into the first couple of months of my freshman year of college. I joined a beer-drinking fraternity, picked up my books as little as possible, and looked to assimilate into the college social culture. However, choices in college usually carry greater moral implications and as I made some bad decisions, I began to carry heavier feelings of guilt and shame. I hit my emotional bottom one afternoon in early November while lying alone on my dorm room bed, thinking about my life and some awful choices I had recently made.

Two days later, I noticed a poster in my dorm advertising a meeting to be held that evening. The meeting was being sponsored by Campus Crusade for Christ. The word Christ caught my attention and I sensed something pulling me to attend the meeting. Although I knew I would be uncomfortable, I felt like I had to go.

Ten students showed up. The speaker, Rick, was on the staff of Campus Crusade. He gave an interesting talk about the uniqueness of Christ. Although his points were clear, what really made an impression on me was the way he conducted himself when some of the students began to interrupt his talk with distracting questions. There was a peace and confidence about him while under pressure that painted quite a contrast to how I was feeling that night.

At the end of the meeting we were asked to fill out a comment card and indicate if we wanted more information about following Christ. Although I feared getting into a religious conversation because I knew so little about it, a person with the peace and confidence I observed in Rick seemed to me to be the exact type of person I needed to help me think through my feelings of guilt. So I turned in my comment card with a request for more information.

Rick stopped by my room the next day. We exchanged background information and found that we had a lot in common. Rick exuded trustworthiness and the qualities of peace and confidence were again evident in his life. Before I knew it, I was telling him my story and describing the guilt and shame I was feeling. Rick listened carefully and offered some encouraging words. He then turned the conversation to what he said was the root cause of my problem. And for the first time in my life, I heard the story of God's provision to forgive me of my sin and to help me with my life. I didn't need to be convinced of my need for forgiveness. And so that afternoon, I bowed my head, but more importantly, my heart and asked Christ to forgive me.

Rick and I became friends and he would stop by my room regularly to offer help in growing as a new Christian. As I grew, I began to experience the peace that I had observed in Rick's life the first night I met him. I also felt clean inside. Throughout my high school years and more so during those first few weeks of college, I lived with a gnawing sense of guilt and shame for my attitudes, words, and actions. I now was experiencing forgiveness for my sin and was learning to confess my sin to God as I became aware of it which gave me the clean-on-the-inside feelings.

Perhaps the most noticeable change I experienced that could be observed by others was the sense of direction and purpose that was now a part of my mindset. For years, I had wandered through life with no idea of where I was headed. I was a follower because I had no concept of the purpose under which all smaller purposes fit. The Bible was showing me that God's overall purpose was for man to love Him, love others, and to help others do the same. No matter whether I was concentrating on my studies, my friends, my family relationships, or my extracurricular activities, I could place all of these smaller efforts under the greater effort of loving God and people. I went from being a follower of men to a follower of Jesus Christ and a leader of men, urging them to come and follow their Savior.

I mentioned at the outset that an accurate summary of my growing up years was that I was a **typical, average, follower**. My life is anything but typical now. **Average** is no longer an accurate description in that God motivates me to seek to excel in all that I do. And with regard to being a **follower**, God has given me a vision for helping to reach the New York metropolitan area through the platform of sports and has equipped me to lead others to help accomplish this mission.

Learning that I matter to God and that He has a role for me to play in His plan for mankind has made all the difference in my life.

George McGovern is on the staff of Athletes in Action (AIA), the sports ministry division of Cru. He is in his 25th year of serving as the chapel leader for the New York Yankees. His responsibilities include leading team Bible studies, serving as personal chaplain for some of the players and their families, overseeing the in-season chapel services, and helping to organize sports-oriented outreaches around the New York metropolitan area. He also gives leadership to five other AIA couples who serve in the New York/New Jersey region.

George received an undergraduate degree in business administration from American University in 1976 and a master's degree in Biblical studies in 1990 from the International School of Theology. George met his wife, Cyndy, at a Bible conference during the summer of 1974. While in college and through their involvement with Cru, they both sensed God's call to missions. They were married in June 1977.

Prior to his current responsibilities, George fulfilled similar duties for six years with the New York Mets and Jets teams. He served the New York Giants in a chaplaincy capacity for 21 years (1996 - 2016). George and Cyndy began vocational Christian work with Cru after graduation from college. They were involved in the campus ministry of Cru for 14 years before switching over to the Athletes in Action effort. George and Cyndy have four married daughters (Kelly, Emily, Mary, and Allison), and reside in Oradell, New Jersey. They are the proud grandparents of Grace Noel, Vincent, Mya, Robbie, J'Rai, Avery, Ty, Maria, Paxton, Claire, Micah, and Margaret.

ဢၧ

A Broken Body and a Broken Heart
By Don Walls

Rock climbing in Colorado is a slow, deliberate yet exhilarating way to spend a few hours. When you reach the top and you gasp that rarefied air, it's a feeling you'll never forget. Coming down can be exciting as well if you don't run out of rope. Like SCUBA diving under ice, it's a sport that's best enjoyed when you're tethered to a friend. As a Young Life leader, in 1988, my friends were three high school members of a group back home in Connecticut.

Young Life is a Christian-based organization focusing on middle school, high school and college age students and is active in all 50 states and 100 countries world-wide. Young Life reaches students through fun-filled weekly meetings in private homes, counseling and outdoor activities.

It was a fabulous trip for everyone and on the last day we climbed a sixteen-hundred-foot rock face. It took us a little longer than anticipated so by the time we reached the summit it was almost seven p.m.

I was the first to rappel down. Something was wrong as I felt the foothold rope slipping through my hands, there was nothing between me and a rocky ledge 70 feet down. I ran out of rope and fell. No time to think about much, I crashed. The impact was so severe I slipped in and out of consciousness. All three boys up on top saw what happened and called for me but all that came out of me were painful mumblings. The second in line rappelled down to the ledge and yelled to the top for help. I felt like I was dead. The rescue operation took almost six hours. I was bleeding internally and after all the exams and tests in the hospital in Boulder, it was determined that I had a ruptured bladder, three broken vertebrae, a fractured hip, and a few other things. In ICU, when they thought they could get through to me, they informed me that my parents were traveling to Florida and couldn't be reached but my brother, Dave, had driven all night to see me.

Dave's divorce was final and hard on the kids, but it left him bitter. He tried to cheer me up but his bitterness kept overcoming him. I tried to tell him how my prayers and those of my friends were helping me and suggested he pray about his situation. My pain medication helped me but there isn't a magic pill you can take to heal the emotional pain Dave had. He was almost yelling at me when he said, "If God was in charge of my life during our marriage, why wasn't He in charge of my wife's as well?" I told Dave to pray, but he left and went home as angry as he was when he came. Lying there thinking about Dave, I realized that he was suffering from isolation from his kids, friends, and even God. I began to pray earnestly for Dave. I felt his emotional trauma overwhelming my physical trauma and God went to work on both of us.

Two weeks later, Dave called to say he had been praying for God to put his broken life together and God performed a miracle of healing in both our lives. By the eighth week I was walking with a cane. If my accident paved the way for my brother and me to get our lives mended, then it was worth all the agony. That's all that mattered.

In lieu of a formal bio, Don Walls offers these 25 items about him on his Facebook page:

1. My middle name is Victor because my father coached a team and when asked if they won, could they name me? My father already had my first name, so they won and chose my middle name.

2. When I was two years old, a huge stable door fell over on me. No broken bones and everything seemed to be OK. Maybe that incident explains a lot of things.

3. I have always wanted to climb in the Himalayas. I can't get enough of seeing big mountains.

4. Growing up, I was exposed to almost every sport on the planet: SCUBA diving, sailing, surfing, riflery, archery, tennis, judo, kayaking, karate, rock climbing…you name it.

5. I've been to every country in Europe, except Ireland.

6. There is nothing more amazing to me than watching my kids grow up, to have seen each of their births and to watch and be involved as they navigate through life. Life is beautiful.

7. I was ENTP (Extraverted iNtuitive Thinking Perceiving) on the Myers-Briggs test and 100% Lion on Leading From Your Strengths.

8. My pet rabbit drowned by hopping into a toilet when I was in third grade. Very traumatic.

9. My favorite concert was The Allman Brothers with warm up acts Lynyrd Skynyrd and Boston.

10. I've met many of my childhood baseball heroes: Roger Maris, Mickey Mantle, Whitey Ford and Yogi Berra. I would liked to have met Babe Ruth (a little before my time, though).

11. My daughter, Linnea, was born in the front seat of the car on the way to the hospital. She came out into the left leg of Sofia's grey sweat-pants.

12. As Lifeguard Captain at Seashore State Park in Delaware, I performed CPR on two people.

13. I've been on top of all the highest mountains in New Hampshire. I climbed Mt. Chocorua when I was only five years old.

14. I like to jump and dive off bridges into the water. Once, I jumped over 100 feet. What a rush!

15. My Dad was a fighter pilot in the South Pacific during WWII. We kids would try on his old uniforms. My favorite picture of my Dad was his pilot picture.

16. Collecting coins is a hobby and I have one certified graded coin of every type minted in the past 160 years. I also have one of most coins from Sweden of every type for the past 135 years.

17. I love history and reading about it, especially American, Swedish and Old West history.

18. I wish I had a few billion dollars to give away to people and causes I believe in.

19. I've spent more than 160 weeks of my life at camps: Summer, Ski, Spring Break, Fall Break, etc.

20. I had my first date and got engaged to my wife at the Hard Rock Café in Stockholm. When I go there now, I wonder how we ever had a deep conversation. It is so loud.

21. I have saved two lives by using the Heimlich Maneuver.

22. I had to learn how to walk all over again and lost 50 pounds in four months following my mountaineering accident in 1988.

23. Had I lived 200 years ago, I would have loved to travel with Lewis and Clark on their expedition across the USA. I always wanted to be a Mountain Man like Jed Smith.

24. I have a multi-colored left eye.

25. I have to take a shower when I get up in the morning. It's a time to get refreshed, pray, get a game plan for the day, etc. A day without a shower is not a day you want to see.

❧◯⟨

Kindness to a Stranger
By Chuck Brockmeyer

By the title you might think it was something I did for someone else, but it's just the opposite, I was the stranger and this is the story of several people who came to my aid when I needed it most.

Herewith, the Bike Trip Adventure/Misadventure:

My friends and I graduated from high school in 1969. To celebrate our freedom, 15 of us planned a motorcycle trip to California. Off we went, full of dreams of camaraderie, new scenery, and wild adventures. But reality is a little more blunt, as we soon found out. First were the mechanical breakdowns. A few of the group dropped out. Then one group wanted to go one way and another group the other, so a split in the camaraderie arrived. One guy lost his belongings, had no more money, and on and on it went until the group dwindled down to just two guys, Jack and yours truly. It was up to us to carry on and make it to California.

So here is one story of many that happened on the road:

I found myself sitting out by the side of the highway somewhere near Blyth (appropriate name) California. There I was with my motorcycle that sputtered to a stop in the middle of the hot California desert and all I had was high hopes for rescue. There was no town or gas station in view in any direction I looked. I wondered out loud, "What's Next?"

Looking at my motorcycle it appeared that the motor had just up and burned out. I was mulling this over when, "Ah ha, Great!" here comes my buddy Jack driving down the highway headed right for me!

I started waving my arms and began jumping up and down. He kept coming and coming and then, then, going and going!

I yelled, "Jack, come back here, what the heck?" I watched stone-faced as he faded slowly into the distance.

To back up a bit on the story, my friend Jack and I were heading back to Arizona from California to meet up with some new friends. It was hot, really hot, so hot I had taken off my shirt, wallet, anything loose and threw it in the old station wagon that Jack had borrowed for this part of the trip. I took off down the highway on my motorcycle with Jack going to follow me in a minute or two.

Now back to the breakdown, here I stood stopped dead in my tracks by the side of the road. I had been riding down the road with just a T-shirt; I had little protection from the sun. Heat blisters started forming on my head and arms as I waited for Jack to come back to help me. Which, of course, wasn't going to happen.

The first help:

After a few hours of waiting, a highway patrolman pulled over and asked "How's it going? Having a bit of trouble?"

"Yes sir, my motorcycle's heat fuses blew up and the bike just ground to a halt. My buddy was following me but he flew right past me without a second glance even though when I saw him coming I was waving my arms like crazy. He had my clothes, my wallet, sleeping bag, everything. He hasn't turned around yet to come back to find me."

The highway patrolman empathized with my predicament and then asked, "So you look hungry, would you like me to take you into town and get you a burger?"

"Super, that would be great" was my relieved response.

He brought me into town and I scarfed down a burger and fries as though it was my last meal. We had some friendly conversation but as it was getting later in the afternoon I told him I had better get back to my bike and wait for Jack in case he returned.

"OK", he said. He drove me back out into the desert to my bike. "I'll check on you later."

That was good news.

The second helpers:

I waited and waited, but no good buddy Jack ever showed up. So, giving in to my fate I began looking around for a place to curl up for the night. As I looked around the rocks and cactus my eye caught sight of an old pickup truck coming down the road slowing down as it came towards me. In the truck were two Mexican fellows who called out, "Hey, what's going on?"

I wondered if this was a safe situation with two strangers I didn't have a clue about, but I told them the story anyway.

"Can we bring you and your motorcycle into town so you can get some help?" they offered.

Even though I hesitated a bit I decided to take them up on their offer, especially since spending the night out in the lonely desert was not a very appealing picture. They had a 2x12 wooden ramp they pulled out the back of the truck and the three of us were able to run the bike up into the truck bed.

We drove into town and saw that everything was closed. They had to go so I told them to drop me off by a gas station, thanked them heartily for their help and chained my bike to a street light nearby. I began to hike around town looking for a place to sleep.

"AHA! A baseball field with dugouts!" A covered dugout should at least give me some protection and privacy. It was a beautiful moonlit night. In spite of all the circumstances I was safe in the dugout and I slept soundly. Even the hard bench seemed comfortable.

The third helper:

The next morning I awoke and in the morning light I noticed a Lutheran Church across the park. "Hey", I thought to myself, "I'm a Lutheran! Maybe they can give me some help."

The pastor said to me, "What can I do for you, young man?"

I replied, "I was left behind by my buddy and he had all my cash. Can I borrow some money to get my motorcycle fixed so I can ride out of here?"

He hesitated. I suppose they get a lot of sob stories at a church, people wanting and begging for money then they just go out and spend it on booze or drugs. Another reason for his pause was I think I looked pretty rough after all what I'd been through, so he wasn't quite convinced I was on the level.

"So then," he asked, "Let me talk with your parents."

I think he was surprised when I immediately said, "OK", and gave him their number. I left the room and they talked for a while. When he came back he had a change of heart and said, "OK, here's a check for $100, try to stay out of trouble." Later my parents showed me a letter the pastor had written to my parents that day. I still have a copy.

"Thanks, so much!" I happily replied. There seemed to be a light at the end of the tunnel.

The forth helpers:

Instead of finding a shop for my bike I decided to hitch-hike to Arizona to find Jack and get his help on fixing my bike. I stuck out my thumb to everyone who drove by. All day, no one stopped, 6-8 hours of standing by the highway in the heat, I was ready to give up. Then here came a car with two people in it and they were pulling over. It was a college professor and one of his students.

He looked me over and said, "I asked my student here if you looked like a safe person to pick up and he told me, "Yah, I think so, he looks like a normal guy to me. Maybe in some kind of trouble. Is that true?"

"Yes, it is."

"Where are you headed?

"Cottonwood, Arizona," I replied.

Driving down the road having some good conversations about all the things that happen on a road trip, then to my amazement, I see Jack's station wagon coming down the highway toward us. "Hey, there's my friend! Can you follow him?"

They did a quick U-turn and set off to catch him. We finally caught up at a rest stop where Jack had pulled in. I got out and was fuming mad. "Didn't you see me there broken down on the side of the road and waving my hands like crazy?" More harsh words, but I'm glad that the Professor stepped in like a referee and calmed me down. After that Jack and I had sort of a happy reunion.

I thanked the professor and student for being there in my time of need. With that Jack and I headed back to town to get my bike fixed.

So it all worked out but certainly wouldn't have without the help from the highway patrolman, the two Mexican fellows, the Lutheran pastor and the professor with his student. I was rescued and eternally grateful.

I have to say my faith in God's help and the good will of others was brought to a new level back in those days and the memory of those great people has stayed with me all these years.

Chuck Brockmeyer Bio

Many years ago, I flopped down on a Swiss hotel bed exhausted after 28 hours without sleep. I had just flown back from a jobsite in Saudi Arabia where a tough but successful project was completed.

As I laid there in beautiful Zurich, it was though I had landed in a fairyland; clean, organized, full of beautiful people and quaint villages. All this was in stark contrast to the land I had just come from where it looked like the world's largest and hottest gravel pit. I looked up from my bed and gratefully thanked God for all the amazing people, helps and miracles He gave us in making this trip a winner. I asked Him, "Lord, thank you for everything. You are my success, but what can I do for you?"

I heard in my spirit a reply, "Tell people what God has done for you." Then He added, "But know, there will be persecution." That has been the root of my stories and a passion of my life.

Here are a few other steps in my life that I consider less consequential but pretty interesting. Right out of junior college I began working for an architect as a draftsman. I had always been involved in drawing and creative writing so I began studying Studio Art at the U of M in Minnesota. There were more jobs and more years as a draftsman and all of a sudden a big break occurred in my work life. I started a 32-year career with a Swiss-owned company. They placed me at the school of Swiss Feed Technology and I earned the title of Feed Production Engineer and later rose to the title of Industry Specialist. The company sent me all around the world putting projects together and selling their equipment.

My wife and I retired together in 2016 and went happily skipping out the door. My helpful and talented wife of 45 years plus our three grown children have all been a wonderful source of stories, learning, and love through the years. My wife and I now pursue nature hikes and road trips and good food while enjoying Florida's great weather.

Notes for your memories of this age:

I MATTER

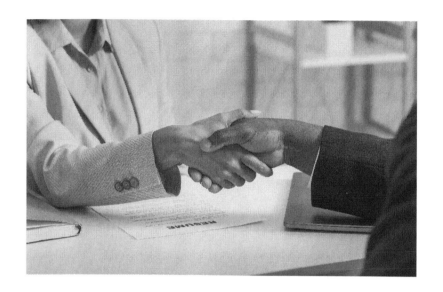

CHAPTER 3

The Age of Responsibility: Adulthood

ॐ

To Hell and Back
By Alonzo Smalls

I was born right in the middle of the Great Depression, not that it made a whole lot of difference to me growing up in Harlem. I hung out with kids like myself. We did everything together, roaming around the neighborhood, making our own fun.

One day, when I was ten years old, we passed a church up around 125th Street. We saw the side door was open, so the three of us decided to explore a place we'd never been before. We entered the empty church. We spotted a staircase and crept up to the balcony. The first thing we noticed was the ceiling. Some words were painted in a big circle and we started to read them out loud: THE . . . WAGES . . . OF SIN . . . IS . . . DEATH . . . BUT, THE GIFT OF . . . GOD . . . IS . . . EEE . . . TERNAL . . . that's as far as we got, when we heard the preacher's voice downstairs. "Hey, what are you boys doing up there?" Oh, oh. "Come on down, come up here by the altar." His voice echoed through the empty church and scared all three of us. We stumbled down the stairs and walked up to the preacher. He said, "You boys were reading the Sinner's Prayer. You know what that means?" He recited the prayer, "The wages of sin is death, but the gift of God is eternal life through Jesus Christ our Lord." Then he said, "Now repeat after me. Dear God..." He went on but we couldn't keep up with him and he finally said, "Just say 'amen' when I'm through." Then he let us go.

That brush with authority soon lost its sting and the three of us joined up with others and shared everything as a group, including bad habits. I soon was smoking and into drugs and by the time I was seventeen, I was mainlining heroin with a $30 a day habit, about $300 in today's economy. Where could I come up with that much money? I started shoplifting and stealing cars. For fifteen years I was mainlining on drugs and in and out of jail for eight of those years. Out of jail and free, it didn't take long to be back on the street with my habit intact.

I went downhill fast and now, at 37 years old, with nothing but dirty clothes on and holed up in a dirty, stinking hotel, I called my momma for help. My sister answered the phone. I said, "Is Momma there?" "You can't talk to Momma", she said. "We're through with your lies and life. I'm taking her down to Brooklyn to live and you can't go there." I pleaded, "I'll change, I've got to get out of this filthy hotel. I've been in here for three weeks. I only have 20 cents to my name." My sister said, "Your name ain't worth 20 cents" and hung up. Oh, Lord, what can I do? My own family won't help me. I have to get out of here and go get me a fix.

I wandered out and down the street. It looked like people were having a church meeting or something right on the street. I tried to get past them when a man said, "Hello, brother, you look like you need a friend." I tried to get through and he said, "I'm Deacon Floyd Williams. Come inside the church with me, there's someone I want you to meet." Who's that? He said, "God is inside, come with me." I needed a fix, but, I went in anyway. There were a few people sitting in the church. I looked around and looked up at the ceiling. In a big circle were the words to the Sinner's Prayer. I said, "This is the same church I was in when I was 10 years old over 25 years ago." As I was read that prayer, I was crying.

Deacon Floyd Williams sort of took care of me for a week or so and I went to that church on Sundays. During the week I didn't change much because I still needed to pay for my drug habit. On the third Sunday in church, the preacher stopped his sermon to say, "There's a brother here today that's hooked on drugs. We have to pray for him right now in the name of Jesus and someone has to stay with him all night in his hotel room to pray for Almighty God to help him with his withdrawal to kick his habit. Deacon Williams, will you do that, tonight?" Deacon Williams said he would.

After church I got in Deacon Williams's car and rapping on the window was a lady. I opened the door and as she got in the front seat with us she said, "Deacon Williams could you give me a lift up to 175th Street?" We started driving and Deacon Floyd said, "This is Alonzo Smalls. Meet Sister Rachel." "Oh, you're the man we prayed for in church today," she said. "Deacon Williams, I don't think you should stay with this man all night tonight and then try to go to your work tomorrow. I have a better idea... Let's take him to Teen Challenge. It's on the way. They have done this before and..." "Teen Challenge? I'm 37 years old", I said. "Oh, that's just their name. They do more than just help teenagers," said Sister Rachel. It was a grueling night but my withdrawal wasn't as hard as I thought it would be. What I didn't know was that in the basement of Teen Challenge was a room full of people praying all night for me. God answered their faithful prayers. Jesus took hold of me that night and changed my life.

For the next two-and one-half years I lived and learned at the Teen Challenge Farm, a Bible school in upstate New York. Then I had a four month-long internship in Los Angeles. On returning to Connecticut, I got a call asking me to start a rehabilitation home for drug and alcohol addicted men. Pivot Ministries was born in Norwalk, Connecticut.

Later another Pivot home began in Bridgeport, Connecticut. Hundreds and hundreds of desperate men have been saved from their addictions, through no medication other than the balm of prayer and the Love of Jesus Christ, and sent out into the world knowing that they mattered to God. I retired from the everyday duties of Pivot Ministries in 2000. It still flourishes under great new leadership. I am 88 years old, as of this writing, and grateful for this opportunity to share the Sinner's Prayer with you, "The Wages of Sin is Death, but the Gift of God is Eternal Life through Christ Jesus our Lord." Do I hear an Amen?

ॐ

On the Fifty Yard Line
By Micheal Barrow

I was born in 1970, and grew up in the small town of Homestead, Florida, and for the next twenty years I was consumed with fame, football and females, but not necessarily in that order. I had an older brother and sister and a younger brother. My parents divorced and my mother married an older man because she was told that an older man would be better for her in raising three children. I didn't have much of a relationship with my stepfather and my real father would take us kids on the weekends, but he wasn't very reliable about that, so I had my share of disappointment.

In the Black community there is a lot of inter-racism between the dark-colored skins and the light-colored skins. It goes back to the days of slavery when the "darkies" worked the fields and the light-colored skins worked in the House. My older brother and sister were dark -colored and I was light-colored. They compounded that separation by telling me I was adopted. Their first names started with a "C" and mine started with an "M", but I had them there because my momma's name was Mae Helen, with an "M", like mine. She was my foundation.

I loved my mom and grandma, I even used my grandma's address as my own for the rest of my life in Homestead. I would go to church with my mom, but only for the free apple juice and cookies. If I ever got out-of-hand, my mom would give me a whoopin', and make me recite Psalm 23 while I was crying my eyes out.

There was a grass field in the "hood". We had small-time teams and we played our version of football. I was never picked first or even second. My older brother, by four years, was a star and I vowed that I would someday be a bigger star. One day he said, "I'll train you to be a better football player, but it won't be easy." My brother knew that when I was little, I was afraid of the dark, so, he made me train at night. He was a senior in high school and I was a freshman. By the time I was a junior, I was playing varsity as an All American linebacker. I was a big star with girls galore and with my lively libido, I was king.

I was a public success and a private failure.

After high school, I got a scholarship to the University of Miami. I was red-shirted, so that didn't allow me to play football my first year. I was depressed and sulking in the locker room when the team Chaplain said, "Are you okay?" We talked and he shared the Gospel with me and said, "All you have to do is say the Sinner's Prayer", which went like this, "The wages of sin is death, but the gift of God is eternal life through Jesus Christ our Lord." The next day in the locker room, I announced, "I am saved." The players in the locker room didn't exactly come on board and, it turned out, I couldn't walk the walk much either, so, by the fall of 1988 I decided I would become a serious Christian. I stopped my lust for a whole two weeks once but that was it. Thank God I never did drugs of any kind but I didn't need to, my other addiction was all-consuming. For ten years I was on a roller coaster of ups and downs.

In 1993, the Houston Oilers drafted me. Houston is a big city and more generous to rising stars like myself. I was a hero and could do no wrong. Four years later I was traded to the Carolina Panthers. As the second-highest paid linebacker in the National Football League from 1988 to 1998 and with never a bad season, things started to fall apart in North Carolina. The press in Charlotte was merciless and never gave me a break. My ego took such a big hit that I even contemplated suicide. At that point in my life what mattered most to me was getting my self-esteem back. I tried, but I knew I couldn't do it myself. I prayed for God to find me a good Christian girlfriend.

After the last game of the season, we all went to a restaurant to celebrate, and, of course, all the cheerleaders were there. However, one of them, Shelley, caught my eye. She was busy but we managed to talk enough to agree to a lunch date. We had a three-hour lunch later and both agreed to meet after I came back from the Christmas break. Back in Charlotte, I went with Shelley to her church. It was a small church and its fiery preacher seemed to be speaking just to me. He had an altar call and I went down and the church people laid hands on me. My arms felt numb. I started crying and repenting. I went to church with Shelley four or five weeks in a row. I cut the church's grass, I fasted for two weeks and I broke up with other girls. Shelley and I became friends focusing only on God and staying chaste for once in my life. I witnessed my changed life to whomever would listen and then turn them over to Shelley or someone in the church for nurturing.

Then I was traded to the New York Giants. What I didn't know at the time was that Shelley had been thinking of moving to New York as well. There is no such thing as coincidence, because mostly it's so perfect that only the spirit of God could pull it off. Thirteen months after our three-hour lunch, Shelley and I were married on January 23, 1999. What a New Year's present. We now have four beautiful children ages 6 to 18.

One of the best things about the New York Giants was getting to know their chaplain, George McGovern, who has written one of the essays in this book. George works with the Giants players and his wife, Cyndy, works with the players' wives to enrich us all with the love of Jesus Christ, as we approach the one-yard line on God's playing field. Even though I left New York for the Washington football team, the Barrow family and the McGovern family are closer than ever.

I don't know my other brothers and sisters who wrote in this book, but what I do know is that we're all God's creation and that's all that matters.

Micheal Colvin Barrow was born on April 19, 1970 in Homestead, Florida. He played football for the Homestead High School Broncos. On scholarship at the University of Miami, he played for the Hurricanes from 1989 to 1992. The team was consensus national champion in 1989 and 1991 and vied for a third national championship in 1992. That year, Barrow was a consensus first-team All-American.

The Houston Oilers drafted Barrow in the second round of the 1993 NFL Draft (47th overall pick). He also played professionally for the Carolina Panthers, New York Giants, Washington football team and Dallas Cowboys. In 2003 with the New York Giants, he led the NFC with 150 tackles. During his 13-year career, he made 1,125 tackles and 43 sacks. Upon retirement from the NFL, he served as the Assistant Head Coach and defensive coordinator for the 2006 season at Homestead High School. He was Linebackers Coach and Special Teams Coordinator at the University of Miami for seven seasons. He joined the Seattle Seahawks as Linebackers Coach in 2015. He has four children: Mikenzi, Kaleb, John Michael, and Michael.

₮)⟨

Let There Be L.I.G.H.T.

By Harlan Rector

Often being told in church, "We have to spread the Good News of Jesus Christ," it somehow fell on deaf ears because I could never buttonhole people on the street or go door to door in my neighborhood.

One Saturday night in the early 1980s, I set my radio alarm for 4:30 a.m. to be part of a team that was winding up a three-day men's religious weekend retreat. At 4:30 sharp I was listening to a radio drama called *Heartbeat Theatre*, stories written with a moral, but not necessarily religious.

As I listened for a few minutes, it hit me. "That's what I'll do," I thought, "I'll tell true stories about how God works in the lives of His People." I was in the radio and TV business, so I knew how to do this. A few days later I called the radio station to ask when they would be airing *Heartbeat Theatre* again. The station manager looked on his radio log and said, "We haven't aired *Heartbeat Theatre* for seven years." "What? That's impossible, I heard it last Sunday morning." "Not true", he said.

That was the beginning of a whole series of "miracles" and how this heavenly inspiration got wings.

Driving home from a meeting of friends who said they would help me put my plan to work, I was thinking aloud, "There should be a name for these dramas." On my windshield I clearly saw the letters **L I G H T**. Whoa! I thought, I wonder that stands for, and then I spoke, "Living In God's Hands Today". I missed the left turn I was making and almost drove onto a golf course, halting traffic in both directions.

On the commuter train one day, I was inspired to write the lyrics for a song to be the L.I.G.H.T. theme. I had never written anything at that point. Amazed by what God was doing I asked a friend at church if he knew any musicians to write the music. He said the only musician he knew was his son's guitar teacher named "Ratso". I called Ratso to tell him about my lyrics and he said, "That's interesting because I just gave up playing hard rock to play in a Christian band with some friends." We met and I showed him my lyrics, he hummed a bit and said, "Come into my studio, I have a song I've been working on that doesn't have words." My lyrics and his song fit so well that not one note was changed. Voila, L.I.G.H.T. had a theme song to begin and end every story. The male vocalist who sings the song, Paul Carney, was the brother of an actor friend of mine, Brian Carney. They both are sons of TV's Art Carney.

There were no radio dramas being produced in New York, where I worked as a voiceover announcer, so I complained daily to my wife that I didn't know how to get anyone to write the stories into a radio drama format. "You were in advertising, why don't you write them", she kept saying. "I was an art director, not a writer," I kept answering. One day on the commuter train to New York, I was inspired to write the first L.I.G.H.T. story, called, Dana. It was a miracle story about our daughter, Dana, and her acute appendicitis in Paris. I continued to write the dramas as stories would come to me from friends. Later I got help from a friend who had been an ad agency writer. The stories were coming from everywhere covering alcoholism, drug addiction, domestic abuse, suicide, health issues and any malady that separates families.

To record these stories, I settled on a small recording studio in New York that was used mostly by the big ad agencies for radio commercials. The owner, Bob, was a New York Italian with a colorful vocabulary, but, whenever we had a session and someone in the studio said something off-color, Bob, who could outdo anyone for cuss words would say, "Hey, none of that language, we're doing God's work today." The studio was a block away from St. Patrick's Cathedral and later on, when Bob was battling cancer, he started dropping by to pray each morning on the way to work. When he was dying in the hospital, he only wanted his assistant, Jed, to be there. One day Jed called me and said Bob wanted me to come to the hospital to see him. He couldn't talk much, so I asked if I could pray for him. He nodded yes. I don't remember what I said, but I remember thinking, If only one person has a change of heart or gets saved, then all the work and words were worth it.

My voiceover talent agency was among the largest in New York and one of the agents offered to cast all the actors who would play the roles in the stories. For all the stories, I employed 178 actors, some multiple times. They had to be paid, the studio got paid for recording and editing, a radio syndicator was retained and ten Christian radio stations had to be paid to air the L.I.G.H.T. stories.

To help pay for what was ahead I held a fund raiser in Old Greenwich, Connecticut, where our church was located. A friend at my church had a big, beautiful house right on Long Island Sound so I asked if I could hold a fundraiser there. He was going to be away for a month so he gave me the keys to his house. I timed the affair when the view of the Sound would be best and had a "High Tea at High Tide". I invited church friends and they brought friends for a huge crowd. Four actor friends came from New York to play roles from four different stories to give the audience a taste of radio drama. A wonderful Sunday afternoon that garnered $13,000 in pledges for L.I.G.H.T. Later, another occasion was held at a huge, beautiful white colonial home in back country Greenwich, Connecticut. The owners' name was White and they were gone but gave their keys to our friend. So, one Sunday afternoon we had "Tea at the White House". The invitation had a mock Presidential seal on it.

My contribution and the donated funds were soon gone so I continued airing L.I.G.H.T on my own. After two years on the air, I wasn't able to produce any new shows, so L.I.G.H.T. went off the air. The stories touched hearts throughout the country, so I thanked God for the inspiration and kept the audio cassettes of each show in a box that went everywhere we went. Thirty-plus years later, a friend suggested I turn the cassettes into CDs and donate them to prison libraries so the prisoners can check out a story or two like they check out a book. I had another friend re-master all the shows for CD production and then had four shows put on each CD. Ten CDs made a beautiful album of all 40 shows.

Now there are albums of L.I.G.H.T. in every prison in Florida and Missouri and half of all the prisons in Texas. When I contacted the Head Chaplain of all the prisons in Illinois he said, "Our prisoners can't have CDs because they cut them in half and use them as sharp weapons... However, they all have smart phones, they could hear your stories on a podcast." One of my sons in Los Angeles converted L.I.G.H.T. to a free podcast so all the prisoners in Illinois can hear and be helped in their rehabilitation. My goal is to reach every prisoner in the country with the inspirational stories of L.I.G.H.T. because they matter to God as well.

Find all the L.I.G.H.T. stories on hrector234.podbean.com.

Notes for your memories of this age:

I MATTER

CHAPTER 4

The Age of Action:
Work / Career

€™™

Lemonade 2
By Harlan Rector

In Chapter One I said our parents took my brother and me with them everywhere they went, including church on Sunday. I didn't realize it at the time but one of the songs we sang in Sunday school would shape my way of thinking. It was a simple song that said, *"Jesus loves the little children, all the children of the world, red and yellow, black and white, they are precious in His sight. Jesus loves the little children of the world."* Although I never met any red, yellow or black children, I figured if it was good enough for Jesus it was good enough for me. Most of my growing up was in the 1940s, when a handshake sealed a deal and it didn't matter what color the other hand was. Being born on Valentine's Day, with all those loving hearts floating around, may have something to do with the fact that anyone I ever met became my friend. My mother lovingly called me her "Comic Valentine". In order to live up to that title I began to see humor in everything, but the class clown doesn't always get the last laugh.

Later, working as an art director in the largest advertising agency in Detroit, I heard from other creatives that it was rating time. Rating time in an ad agency? Here's how it worked. Our group's head art director, Bill, would rate each AD and send it to the creative director who would then go over Bill's rating with each one of us separately. My turn came with Harry the creative director, a very nice, soft-spoken guy in his late 40s. "Harlan", he said, "Bill has rated you outstanding in every category except one. Outstanding is reserved for the Chairman of the Board." I said, "Every category except one, which one?" Harry said, "Accepts criticism. What do you have to say about that?" Here's where I learned that words mattered. Overwhelmed by all the outstanding's, I said, "Harry, with all those outstanding ratings, maybe I shouldn't have to." Harry didn't say anything and I felt terrible. Shortly after, Bill quit to take another job and they promoted me to Head Art Director. Everything was fine until the agency brought in a creative director from New York who wanted to change things. I was demoted. I was handed a big, sour lemon. This one would take a lot of sugar to make lemonade.

The following is an excerpt from my book "Once Upon a Corner in Detroit". It explains one of the ways I've been blessed throughout my life and takes place a day or two after my demotion.

One day, in 1971, a copywriter and I sat in my office trying in vain to create a print ad for one of Rockwell's divisions. We were getting nowhere and needed a break. With a drawing pad in one hand and Sharpie magic marker in the other, I doodled a caricature of the writer. I remembered trying to do caricatures at a previous ad agency, but I don't remember them being very good. I was surprised how well this one turned out. I stuck it up on the wall. My office soon became the most popular place in the agency. Anyone who stopped by my office was immortalized — the four walls decorated to the ceiling with caricatures.

Inspired by my new-found talent, I began taking a drawing pad and a Sharpie or two with me everywhere I went. For lunch one day, I wandered into a restaurant near my office. Everything in Detroit pertained to automobiles so the restaurant was aptly named The Steering Wheel. Off in the corner near the bar, WJR was remotely broadcasting. The 50,000-watt radio station was conducting its daily, hour-long interview show *Focus*.

Any celebrity on a publicity tour hawking a movie, book or just happened to be in town, was interviewed on *Focus* by JP McCarthy, the Voice of Detroit. Known by all as JP, he could talk on any subject and with such personal delivery his listeners felt they were sitting with him at their kitchen table for lunch. For a while, JP had both morning and evening drive-time shows, five times a week. That was unprecedented for Detroit radio. Later, he dropped his evening show to concentrate more on his morning show and the noontime *Focus* show.

Back to that day at The Steering Wheel, I was sitting at the bar, close to the radio show already in progress with an interview ending. I felt compelled so I grabbed my pad, uncapped my Sharpie, and drew a caricature of McCarthy. After the show, JP and his producer came over to the bar next to where I was sitting.

I introduced myself and showed JP his caricature. He laughed. "Nice to meet you Harlan, do you have a job or do you just hang around bars for a living?" I smiled. "I'm an art director at Campbell-Ewald across the street. I just happened to be here for lunch."

JP looked over at his nodding producer. "What do you think about coming to The Steering Wheel every day to draw caricatures of our guests on the show?" he asked.

What could I say? "Wow," I answered.

My Selfie Caricature

The very next day I was on the *Focus* show and for a couple of years I spent my lunch hour drawing more than 100 celebrities as they were being interviewed. When an interview was over, I'd meet the guest, ask them to autograph the caricature and Clarence Baker, the restaurant owner, would thumbtack it to the wall — the goal was to replicate the décor of Sardi's in New York. When WJR decided to broadcast *Focus* from their own studio, I took the caricatures off the wall. I can tell which ones were done at The Steering Wheel by the tiny thumbtack holes in the corners of the paper.

The interviews were about 16 minutes, so I had to draw quickly to catch an expression or feature to produce their likeness. Every line or stroke had to be right because you can't erase a Sharpie magic marker. In WJR's studio I decided to make two identical caricatures of every celebrity. I gave the guest their own and asked them to autograph the other for me. No one ever objected and some of them wrote messages. Only two celebrities were unhappy with their caricature but graciously signed them anyway.

To be continued in Chapter 6.

ஐ෬

For the Love of Writing
By Tracy Tripp

One of the beautiful aspects of life is that we are always changing and transforming as new experiences become a part of our story. We never have to feel stuck in a place or a personality. We can go from an "I can't" person to an "I will" person. Most of the transforming experiences are small, and the change in us happens in increments too minute to measure. Others are more noticeable, like a move or a marriage. But if we are lucky, one of those experiences is due to an accomplishment or success we have strived to achieve. For me, this accomplishment was writing my first novel.

I grew up on a dairy farm and was one of seven children. There was little income to go around and even less confidence. Yes, I said confidence. It is a gift that some are born with, and others are taught. It is a gift that can take people to places to which they might not otherwise be capable of traveling.

I wasn't always aware of my lack of confidence compared to others. My parents, who were both wonderful, had been beaten down by the lack of income, endless work, seven fighting children, and the bad luck that seemed to follow them. Eventually, my parents chalked it up to the Sheehan (my maiden name) Curse. If it could go wrong for us it would, and for some time, I believed that we were just not meant to be successful or dream big.

College was an iffy goal for most of us and wasn't pushed upon us at all. Even so, several of my siblings went on to two- or four-year programs. I became determined and with much effort and several jobs, I worked my way through my bachelor's and eventually, my master's, obtaining a degree in teaching. I was determined to leave the Sheehan Curse behind and was ready to make a new start with a positive mindset.

I taught in various positions and then stopped to raise my family. While at home, I began to write. Why do people write when only the smallest percentage of people succeed in making this a profession? Most would say, we have stories within us that must come out. But for me, it was more than just that. Writing to me was about accomplishing something I thought might only be for someone else to accomplish— someone with a better background, more knowledge, more confidence, more of whatever I often thought I was missing. Writing my first novel was telling myself that my dreams were attainable.

My first novel started as a short story as I toyed with its idea. Like a seed, more words sprouted and then spread across the pages until eventually, I hit that moment when I knew it was possible. I would be able to say I was an author.

The day came that I finally got to type the words, The End. Shortly after, I was ripping open a box and holding my dream in my hands. The feeling was incredible. But then it had to be advertised and put out there for others to judge. Was I scared about what people would think of my story? Did I wake up sweating the night before it was officially released? Definitely.

I wasn't sure what would happen the day it became available but will admit I imagined myself sitting on Oprah's couch being heralded for my amazing story-telling abilities. In my mind, I envisioned agents wanting to see more of my work. I might have taken a few flights across the country to attend book signings, and possibly I needed a security guard in a couple of my imagined scenarios. But that's not quite how the story unfolded. My book went public, my friends and family gobbled it up, sent kind texts and emails, and some even invited me to be a guest author at their book clubs. Little moments that teased me before falling short of the imagined ones.

During my years of writing, I have ridden my roller coaster made of small hills and little valleys and learned one thing. Achieving one's dream should always be about becoming his or her very best self and not necessarily the very best at what you do. This rating is generally an opinion anyway, and there will never be a time when everyone's opinions are the same. Therefore, if you wait for the whole world to decide you are the best, you will most likely be let down. If your very best self is an award-winning author, then yes, you should attain that goal. And if your very best self is publishing a few good books that you are proud of, you have achieved amazing things. You have achieved being the very best you and being brave enough to reach for the stars in your universe.

My success is two-fold. Yes, I accomplished my writing goal, but in that journey, I was blessed with another accomplishment that came in unexpected ways. I learned to feel successful in attaining the goals within my bubble of ability. Will I keep trying for the next best seller? Of course, but the actual achievement has already been realized.

Tracy Tripp was born and raised in Potsdam, New York. She attended the State University of New York at Oswego where she earned her degree in teaching, and then earned her Master's degree in education from Buffalo State College. After one particularly cold winter in Buffalo, she and her husband decided living a bit

farther south would be nice, so they moved to Richmond, Virginia where Tracy taught middle school along with various other grades, and they began to raise their family. After eighteen years, she moved to Jacksonville, Florida with her husband and three children. Tracy likes to write stories about the human spirit and the challenges that shape them, but is also open to any whimsical idea that comes her way. Her books include Parting Gifts, Still Life, Something Like a Dream, and The Wealthy Frog. The sequel to Something Like a Dream, Awaken, a children's book titled Sammy the Snowman, and a thriller, tentatively titled White Noise Whispers, co-authored with Edward Mickolus, are all in the works. Tracy also has a blog that includes interviews with Jacksonville's homeless. Read more about her and her works at tracytripp.com

ॐ♋

Poetry
By Patricia Daly-Lipe

My writing began in 7th grade at The Bishop's School in La Jolla, California. I wrote for SAHATIKA (sees all, hears all, thinks it knows all) newspaper. From there to Vassar College where I wrote for *The Miscellany News*. Then my first real job after returning from living in Europe was writing for *The Evening Star* newspaper in Washington, D.C. I was supposed to answer the phone, take the call from a reporter on the scene, and transcribe it into an article. The problem was I had been speaking French and Italian for two years and could not understand the reporters. The reason? Yes, it was English, but they spoke with a southern accent and so rapidly, I kept asking them to repeat! So, the newspaper transferred me. My new job? Writing obituaries!

To return to my passion for writing: It didn't begin with poetry. It was people and their stories that begged for my attention; hence my philosophy, history is biography. The personal perspective is what fascinates me. My degrees are in philosophy, not history. This leads me to Aristotle who wrote that poetry was more philosophical than history since poetry dealt with the universal and history with the unique facts or epics, i.e., the particular. Poetry develops within the reader an appetite for metaphysics since it conveys from a personal perspective the human experience. Remember, philosophy was my major!

Ultimately, I came to poetry.

Poetry appeals to the senses. It celebrates feelings. Robert Frost observed that, "No tears in the writer; no tears in the reader." "A poem begins with a lump in the throat." Poetry reflects passion. Poetry comes from the heart. Joseph Campbell counselled, "We need more poetry that reveals what the heart is ready to recognize."

One of the most powerful mimes of what is life is sound. Take the "motion" out of "emotion". Music has that power. Music is motion. Life is motion. There is a certain affinity between musical rhythm and literary rhythm and we find this affinity in poetry. There is rhythm in its repetition/rhythm/meter/movement/harmony. Poetry reflects motion as it dances with words. Poetry values each word. It is compact and, as such, poetry is a great disciplinarian.

To me, writing poetry is a challenge. It is most difficult to write since its literary lyrics, the quality of its language, is condensed as a vapor into a liquid.

But remember, man is both creature and creator. Creative energy creates. The journey never ends. So, give it a try. I did!

A Poetic Meditation

On this earth, there is oneness.

A rhythmic flow, a great symphony that is life.

Trees with roots, stems and leaves

Shells, fins, furs and wings, all living things.

Each has a purpose and to each, an end

And then . . . a new beginning.

Let us recapture the imagination of a child

See once more the mystery, beauty and joy of God

Playing within and behind, beyond and above.

Unite with the intimacy of commitment.

Trust takes time

But the gift is there . . . waiting.

Literary Lady Dr. Patricia Daly-Lipe is an artist and speaker who has written ten books:

- *Miami's Yester' Years: Its Forgotten Founder Locke Tiffen Highleyman*
- *Messages From Nature (a collection of short stories about animals, the high seas, and nature)*
- *A Cruel Calm: Paris Between the Wars (historical fiction)*
- *Myth, Magic and Metaphor: A Journey into the Heart of Creativity*
- *All Alone: Washington to Rome (a biography)*
- *La Jolla, A Celebration of Its Past*
- *Historic Tales of La Jolla*
- *Patriot Priest: The Story of Monsignor William A. Hemmick, The Vatican's First American Canon*
- *Helen Holt: Memoir of a Servant Leader*
- *Horse Tales: Teddy and Just'n Come to an Understanding*

The La Jolla book was the Winner of the San Diego Books Awards in 2002. A Cruel Calm (1st edition: Forbidden Loves) won the 1st Runner-Up for Fiction JADA Trophy, the USABookNews.com Finalist Award, and in 2013 won First Prize for historical fiction Royal Dragonfly Book Award. She was named Author of the Year 2016-2017 by the International Association of Top Professionals, which gave her a Lifetime of Achievement and Success award in 2017.

She has written for the Evening Star newspaper in Washington, D.C., the Beach and Bay Press including La Jolla Village News in California, and The Georgetowner and Uptowner newspapers in Washington, D.C., as well as several magazines across the country.

Her presentations have covered all aspects of writing for literary groups as well as colleges and universities.

In her "spare" time, Patricia has been rescuing thoroughbred horses. In the late 1970s and 1980s, she raised, raced and showed them.

ℰⓇ

There's Always Hope
By Greg Barry

In my younger days, I worked as an emergency medical technician (EMT) in a busy hospital in Santa Monica, California.

It was interesting, exciting, stressful, fulfilling, and too many times, tragic. Our hospital was a paramedic base station receiving the most serious of ambulance runs. There were many situations involving life and death moments. The staff physicians, nurses, EMTs and ancillary staff worked hard to stabilize or resuscitate patients depending on the need. We were mostly successful but sometimes we weren't.

We were well trained to manage our emotions for both successes and failures. We had to be able to move on to the next patients and their medical issues. There was no time to ruminate over difficult situations and unavoidable tragedy. Our jobs demanded that we stay centered, agile and nimble because anything could come rushing through the door at any moment.

I have many indelible memories from my years as an EMT. There were gang-related shootings, stabbings, near-drownings, cardiac arrests, traffic accidents, psychiatric situations, burn victims, marine-related attacks, celebrity encounters, abuses of various kinds, and much more.

But of all the situations I dealt with, the one I think about most involved one of our regular patients who had been found down in a park as he often was, and as always, he was inebriated. The coastal city of Santa Monica was the end of the rainbow for many people around the country and when they got there, many fell upon hard times. As a result, there was a high indigent population many of whom had substance abuse issues to further complicate their lives.

We can call him Allen. I had probably dealt with him 5-6 times in the past; all related to alcohol abuse. We checked him into the emergency department (ED), took his vital signs, checked his blood alcohol level and started an IV to rehydrate him. After a couple of hours, he would be ambulatory and he would check himself out, until next time.

The next time Allen was brought in via ambulance he received the usual treatment in the ED. Then when he was buffed up and ready to go he asked me my name. That was a first. He didn't remember me from past ED visits but he'd never asked me a question before, much less a personal one. He told me he needed help. I looked into his still blood-shot eyes and tried to determine if he was being honest. As an ED worker it's easy to become jaded because so many patients try to take advantage of you.

Of course I knew he needed help but I was impressed that he actually verbalized it. I went to our department resource center and picked out a couple of appropriate booklets for him. He thanked me and then left the hospital.

A few months later Allen was back. He was brought in for the usual problem. I checked him in as usual. He was treated by a physician and received his IV fluids. A few hours later he was ready to go. I didn't remind him of our last encounter. I acted as if he was a regular patient. In a soft voice he called me over by name. He told me he remembered me from last time and that he still needed help. I agreed. I got him the same set of booklets as before to take with him.

I'm not a substance abuse counselor but I told him that if he was to be successful he would need to be ready to change and he would need to commit to improving his life and that a good way to start would be to attend the free substance abuse classes sponsored by the city for the homeless. I told him I had confidence he could succeed. I wasn't really sure if he could succeed or not but at the time it was clear to me that the man needed some encouragement.

About a year later, Allen was in the ED again. But this time he wasn't there for an alcohol-related matter. He had simply cut his finger slicing vegetables at the local homeless shelter where he now worked and needed some stitches. When he saw me he smiled. He looked better. He shared that he hadn't had any alcohol for a while and because of his willingness to help others at the shelter they kept him on as a resident, even providing him a small stipend for essentials.

He thanked me and told me I was the first person in a long time who believed in him and was willing to help. I smiled back and told him how impressed I was at all of his progress. I also felt guilty because I hadn't really extended myself too much and I didn't think about him after he had left the ED the last time. But apparently, our brief personal moments together were enough to help get him on a better track.

Not long after that I left the hospital for another job at UCLA Medical Center. I never saw Allen again. I sometimes wonder how he did. I like to think he kept improving his life and leave it at that.

For me, it taught me how sometimes it's really the little things in life that matter most. A few words of encouragement and support is all some people need to get over a hump in their lives and to miss those opportunities, as subtle as they may be, can be a difference maker to a person in need.

ℰ)Cℛ

My Life's Work
By George McGovern

Have you ever been captured by a big idea? Have you ever been burdened to do something that you could not accomplish by yourself? Or, has God ever put a "mission" on your heart that you could not brush off?

I bumped into these questions during my first year on staff with a Christian ministry, Campus Crusade for Christ (now known as CRU). I was assigned to the University of Georgia CRU staff team and was trained in ministry skills by a seasoned staff guy, Garry Kiker. On one of our standing training appointments, Garry asked me to describe the vision God had placed on my heart. I answered the best I could at that moment. I said I wanted to help fulfill the commission that Jesus gave to His close followers. It's recorded in the gospel of Matthew in the Bible. In essence, Jesus commissions His followers to "make disciples of others such that they, too, observe His teachings". Garry affirmed my answer, but then challenged me to put some "meat on those bones". He encouraged me to pray and think about a life vision that would reflect my life experiences, my talents, and God's will.

I followed Garry's directive and spent time alone, praying and wrestling with these three life components: my experiences, my talents, and God's will. Some ideas began to crystallize. One of my "life experiences" was that I grew up in the New York City metropolitan area. Another was the lack of ever hearing, while growing up, the good news that God had sent His Son to die on a cross to pay the penalty for my sin. As to my God-given gifts and abilities, I identified some that would serve me well if I accepted leadership responsibilities in the CRU organization. And as to connecting with God's will, I knew that He wanted His followers, and me specifically, to be engaged in the mission of convincing and teaching men and women to embrace Jesus as their Savior and Lord.

As these ideas took on greater clarity in my heart and mind, they converged with a deeper awareness that God was directing my life. The main components of this direction were New York City, leadership responsibilities, and "making disciples". As a result when an opening came for the position of Campus Director for CRU at Rutgers University (located in a suburb of New York City) Cyndy and I immediately applied for it. We were given the green light and moved there in the summer of 1979. We went to work with a small staff team and tried many approaches and various outreach events and strategies to present the claims of Christ to the 30,000 students. For 12 years we saw ourselves as farmers who were weeding the field, planting seed, watering the seed, and harvesting as some seed reached maturity. The work was arduous, but we knew we were in the center of God's will for our lives…leading evangelistic and discipleship efforts in the New York City area.

During the time at Rutgers, our family grew to include four daughters. Perhaps that is, in part, the reason that I accepted a change in assignment in 1990 to work in all-male locker rooms. I was asked to switch to the Athletes in Action branch of CRU and join their division that worked with professional sports teams. The goal was the same—winning, building, and then sending people to help fulfill the great commission. Only now we would be working with pro athletes, coaches and their wives. This new responsibility fit right in line with the picture God had given me of helping to reach the New York City area for Christ. But it had the potential to expand our platform and, thus, impact a wider audience since professional athletes and coaches are highly respected in this culture.

We began our pro sports team ministry with the New York Jets and Mets. My activities included leading the pre-game chapel services for both teams, conducting players and coaches weekly after-work Bible studies, and meeting one-on-one with players and coaches to help them grow in faith and character. After four years, I was asked to add the chapel responsibility for the New Jersey Nets (NBA) to my job description. After six years of working with the Jets and Mets teams, we were transferred to the Yankees and Giants. So, our pro sports ministry experience includes six seasons with the Jets and Mets, five with the New Jersey Nets, 20 with the New York Giants, and we're in our 25th year with the New York Yankees.

Over these 31 years, I've had the privilege of conducting scores of outreaches in the New York metropolitan area where athletes and coaches have shared their stories of faith in Jesus Christ and the difference that He has made and continues to make in their lives. Through our partnerships with various church and para-church ministries, we've helped these ministries expand their "reach" into their communities and youth populations. I've had the opportunity to train scores of high school and collegiate coaches in using their position of influence to encourage their athletes in faith and character. God has opened doors for me, locally, to mentor younger sports team ministers and thereby increasing the number of athletes and coaches who are finding Christ and growing in that relationship. The vision God painted in my heart as a young campus minister in Athens, Georgia has blossomed into reality in the New York City metropolitan area.

During my years with the NY Giants, the team competed in three Super Bowl games. They won two of them (SB XLII, SB XLVI). It's common knowledge that the players, coaches, and staff of the winning team receive rings commemorating their achievement. I, too, received a Super Bowl ring for both of those victories. But the irony is that I didn't play one down in any game. I didn't offer one coaching tip to any player nor did any coach ask me for help in any of their game planning. None of the team's scouts asked for my recommendation as to whom the team should draft. None of the trainers or doctors sought my advice on how to treat injured Giants players. I didn't do one thing to contribute to the team's on-field success. And yet, the owners of the team gave me two Super Bowl rings.

Getting something good you didn't earn. That's a good definition of grace. When I think of the rings, I think of grace…getting something good that I didn't deserve. And that makes me think of forgiveness and eternal life. You see, the cross is the place where Jesus Christ, who didn't do anything wrong, bore the penalty for all the wrong that I have done and will do. His death satisfied the debt that I owed God for my wrong-doing. Because Jesus took my debt and paid it by dying on the cross, I'm forgiven of that debt, and thereby granted the promise of eternal life... grace...getting something good that I don't deserve.

Every time I look at those rings, I'm also reminded of the vision God planted in my heart. Remember, they are the Super Bowl rings of the world champion New York Giants. I've been blessed to be involved in the work of God in the New York metropolitan area. The interest, the burden, the conviction I have to be a "farmer" in God's Big Apple field is of His doing. He adopted me into His family, trained me to be a laborer, and then placed me in this particular field. When I say "my vision", I'm really talking about God's vision, the vision He had (and still has) for my life. Until He calls me home, I'm burdened to press on and labor in the New York metropolitan area.

What idea or mission has God placed on your heart?

Be careful. You may just be in for the thrill of your life!

ഔരു

A Bank That Lends a Hand as Well as Money
By Diane Machaby

In July 2002, while I was working as the only employee at Habitat for Humanity in St. Augustine, Florida, a Bank of America associate called to schedule a team-building experience on the United Way's Day of Caring scheduled for September 6, 2002. We were thrilled to have a group of 20 volunteers willing to help in the heat of the summer. Without delay, I sent the coordinator our affiliate's organizational information, volunteer information, and a map to the build location. So, the group was lined up well in advance of their scheduled volunteer day, nearly two months ahead of time.

Meanwhile, a Bank of America employee in St. Augustine, Qwanda Mitchell, applied for and was approved for a Habitat for Humanity home. Qwanda and her children were thrilled with the possibility of having their own three-bedroom, two-bath home and immediately began logging the required 400 hours of sweat equity on the build site and attending the various homeownership workshops. They were determined to get into their new home as soon as they could.

On Saturday, September 6, the Bank of America volunteers that had been scheduled in July arrived on the site. They were willing to perform whatever tasks our construction leader had for them on any house we had under construction that day. Little did they know, nor did we realize, that the 20 volunteers would be assigned to build the home for one of their own employees, Qwanda Mitchell!

I was working in the office the morning that the Bank of America volunteers arrived and decided to drive out to the build site later that day. I had heard that a business friend of mine from Jacksonville, Mac Holley, the bank's Vice President for the North Florida region, was going to be volunteering on the build.

When I arrived, I heard the news that the Bank of America team members were building a home for one of their colleagues. I was shocked that things had worked out this way but at the same time I was very thrilled. I could not have planned this build any better, if I had done it myself… which I had not!

While we were eating lunch, I talked to Mac Holley about the possibility of Bank of America sponsoring the home for Qwanda Mitchell and her family. He said he would like to see the company do that and he would be in touch in the next few days after he discussed it with the corporate office. I thanked him and headed back to the office.

When I arrived at work the very next day I was elated to find a message on the answering machine from Mac Holley who said that Bank of America would be happy to sponsor the home for the Mitchell family to the tune of $50,000!

Throughout the next few months, the employees continued to volunteer on the Mitchells' home and on the day of the dedication, there wasn't a dry eye in the house. Qwanda and her two children were now moving into a brand new, three-bedroom home that her family, friends, and co-workers had helped to build.

Within two weeks, Qwanda's Bank of America colleagues hosted a house-warming celebration for her. At the event, she and her children received most everything they needed to furnish and decorate their new home. It is amazing how God lined this up for all of us: Qwanda, her family, her Bank of America co-workers, and even for our Habitat for Humanity affiliate. God Is So Good!

This article appeared as "Bank Employees Help Out" in Diane Quick-Machaby's When God Showed Up: Recognizing His Hand in Our Lives Charleston, NC, 2017.

Diane Quick-Machaby is a native Floridian living her entire life in North and Central Florida. She has two grown daughters and has lived in the Jacksonville area for over 25 years

After being a stay-at-home mom, room mom, PTA mom, and community activist, Diane got involved in non-profit work in the early 1990s. Over the past 25 years, she's worked in the City of Jacksonville's Keep Jacksonville Beautiful Programs, Habitat for Humanity in Jacksonville and St. Augustine, and most recently with Home Again St. Johns, an agency that works directly with the Homeless of St. Johns County.

In 2015 Diane and her husband started their own business, Art 4 Charities, LLC, which partners with nonprofits worldwide in their fundraising efforts.

Diane and Terry Machaby live with their long-haired calico cat, Scarlett, in Nocatee, Florida, and attend Crosswater Community Church

ॐ⃝છ

A Creative Sandwich
By Sheila Weinstein

When I turned 20, I couldn't drink legally or vote, but I could marry, and I did. At 30, I was the mother of three. At 40, I realized I'd probably arrived at the half way mark and took to my bed after the birthday cake. Successive decades brought their joys and sorrows. In my 60s, my husband, a practicing physician, was diagnosed with dementia. It took eight years for the disease to run its course.

I moved to New York City alone, frightened and lonely. What helped me through the sorrow and bewilderment of losing the man I loved all my life was my passion for music and writing. Depression brought me the gift of songs. I wrote 11 of them over the next years. I became a docent at Carnegie Hall, taking visitors from all over the world on tours every week. And, due to serendipitous circumstances, I played there one glorious night. I wrote a book about learning to live alone after 42 years of marriage. At 75 I turned the book into a play.

To be engaged in something joyful that takes me out of myself and yet into my deepest self continues to keep me alive and well.

The immutable facts are that at this point in our lives we are bound to lose connection with beloved friends and family, and we are more prone to illness ourselves. So, then, to what can we turn, or perhaps, run for consolation and solace? I say: Creativity, in any of its forms. If we happen to be artistic, we can create art and be elevated by it in spite of our circumstances, and, in the process, touch other lives. But, opening to others' creative works can also lift us above our personal pain. When I have a sad day, I take myself to a museum and sit in front of some of the grandest paintings ever created, knowing that those artists, too, were translating their pain, love, and loneliness into their work. It makes me feel connected to something grander than myself.

I define creativity broadly. For instance, at a book signing I talked about the value of creativity in our lives to a group of women who were in various stages of grief. One woman stood and said: "Well, that's fine, but some of us are not creative." I said to her: "Can you make a sandwich?" She said, "Of course!" I said, "Then make one, or two, or ten, put it in a bag with some other goodies, take it out on the street and feed someone who's hungry. That's creative. It will nourish someone else and you as well."

If you don't believe you are creative, all you have to do is seek ways to help others. Find the need and creatively fill it. Deliver an anonymous basket of food, tape a little gift on the door of an aging neighbor. Offer to read to someone in a hospital. The possibilities are endless.

Whatever your creative interest, stay attached to it. Your life will be richer for it.

I wish you a healthy and creative life!

Photo by Joe Henson

Sheila Weinstein is a writer and pianist who grew up in New Jersey, was educated in New York City at Barnard College and obtained her MA degree in Music from Trinity University in San Antonio, Texas where her husband was head of the Division of Ophthalmology at the University of Texas Health Sciences Center. She taught piano privately there and when the family moved to West Virginia she began writing while continuing to teach piano at the Creative Arts Center of West Virginia University, and in her home. Their children grown and on their own, she and her husband moved to Florida where her husband opened a private practice. His practice ended when he was diagnosed with dementia. Several years later, when he entered a dementia facility, Sheila moved to New York City, alone for the first time in her life, having met her future husband when she was 16. There she decided to write about her journey and turned it into a book called Moving to the Center of the Bed: The Artful Creation of a Life Alone, which she hoped might help others. While writing the book, she took advantage of everything New York City had to offer, most especially becoming a docent at her beloved Carnegie Hall. In 2008 she was privileged to play her own compositions in Carnegie Hall's Weill Recital Hall. In 2014 she returned to Florida where she lives today. She has given courses at the Osher Lifelong Learning Institute on memoir writing, aging, and Carnegie Hall. She describes her docent work at Carnegie Hall as the most meaningful experience of her life. She is now 83 and writing a novel about Frederic Chopin.

&)CR

What's in a Name?
By Ed Mickolus

A friend is fortunate that her great grandfather left a good draft of her lineage. Mine—on both sides—is pretty much oral history. I've always been happy to trace back to my parents! For me, that's enough. They provided me with a model of a loving, albeit small, family. I hope Susan and I have been able to provide that environment to our only child, our accomplished daughter.

I wasn't just my parents' only child. Of the four Catholic Mickolus brothers of my Dad's generation, I was the only child. There just isn't that much to trace!

So our nuclear family focused on getting meaning from our faith and our works, a theme you'll see in some of my other essays in this volume.

Many people derive part of their meaning from understanding where they fit in their ancestry, developing extensive family trees (I once met a person who had 200,000 entries on his; I suspect he can trace back to Lucy!), spitting in a cup to give 23&me a DNA sample, pouring through musty volumes on Ellis Island, and attending large family reunions where they try to figure out what a 23rd cousin seven times removed means.

I fell into information about my heritage through inadvertence and the doggedness of FBI investigators.

On my first day at CIA's Counterterrorism Center, I handed the tracer (view him/her as a biographer who works with classified information) a bunch of Arabic names. Thinking that my near-unique last name (Go ahead. Google it. I'll wait.) was also to be traced, he produced a document that said "Division ____ has a file." So off I went to that Division, whose file simply said "The FBI has a file on your Dad." Armed with my Dad's death certificate, I FOIAd them, and after a two-year wait, the FBI produced several pages of Bureau-speak interviews.

Apparently in 1953, my Dad, who was working as an engine engineer for Ford, was spotted by a McCarthyite snoop who questioned why Dad was reading a Ford transmission manual. "This guy's got a Lithuanian name. That's part of the commie USSR! He's stealing our national security transmission secrets!" So he dimed my Dad to the Bureau, which tasked six field offices and interviewed everyone my parents and grandparents had ever met.

Thanks to their file, I know the name of the boats my grandparents came on, the addresses of every home in which they and my parents lived, their schools, their friends, their interests, and even my date of conception (and how many people can say that? The FBI found that my Dad graduated from a college program on March 28, 1950. I was born on December 28, 1950. I'm guessing they must have celebrated that night!). After all that work, the file never came to a conclusion about commie spying. If the FBI had merely checked the Ford parking lot, they would have seen that Dad drove a 1953 Ford that had a transmission problem...

ᏉᏣᏅ

The Telephone Call
That Changed My Life
By Harvey Hofmann

In February 1973, I was Manager-Technical Communications for Teledyne CAE, headquartered in Toledo, Ohio. Teledyne CAE (a subsidiary of Teledyne, Inc.) manufactured small gas turbine engines for military applications. My responsibilities included advertising, public relations, exhibits, the Technical Publications Department and corporate identity.

Teledyne, Inc., with more than 40 subsidiary companies, had recently published a new Corporate Identity Manual showing how to use Teledyne as the first name of each of their subsidiaries. Whenever I saw misuse of other Teledyne subsidiaries using incorrect identity on advertisements, vehicles, or company signs, I copied them and made 35 mm slides.

Ron Kimler and Associates was the advertising company for Teledyne CAE. Harlan Rector was an associate of Ron Kimler. The two assisted me in producing a 35mm slide presentation of the incorrect use of Teledyne, Inc. corporate identity. With the approval of my boss, I contacted Teledyne, Inc., headquarters in Los Angeles in February 1973. I said I would like to show them samples of what I had found with their subsidiaries incorrectly implementing their new identity program. After I showed the presentation to the Teledyne, Inc. Vice President of Communications, he agreed with me about the problem but advised me that Teledyne Corporate headquarters did not have the staff to follow up.

In March 1973 on a Sunday afternoon in Sylvania, Ohio, Ron Kimler phoned me. He said Harlan Rector, a creative designer for Campbell Ewald Advertising Company, was working on the advertising account of a company that had recently changed their company name and were looking for a corporate identity person. The company was Rockwell International, who had changed their name from North American Rockwell. Harlan Rector recommended me for the position because of the corporate identity presentation I put together for Teledyne, Inc. Kimler gave me Jack Laffin's phone number at Rockwell and wished me good luck.

Jack Laffin was Director of Communications at Rockwell International's corporate headquarters in Pittsburgh, Pennsylvania. I called Jack and arranged an interview with him and his staff to show them my Teledyne, Inc. presentation the following Monday. In our meeting, Laffin advised me that he was interviewing other candidates for the position and he would call me with his decision at a later date.

While I was setting up a Teledyne CAE gas turbine exhibit for the US Navy League in Washington, D.C., the phone rang in our booth. It was Jack Laffin saying that he had made a decision and invited me to join Rockwell International in Pittsburgh. I said I could call Jack on the following Monday when I had returned to Sylvania and give him my answer.

Upon returning to my office on April 23, 1973, I looked at my office surroundings, including Teledyne CAE advertisement copies, exhibit photographs, turbine engine technical data sheets, mounted on a wall. I said to myself if I don't take this job with Rockwell I will be doing my current job for the rest of my life. With this in mind I phoned Jack and accepted the position of Corporate Identity Coordinator for Rockwell International Corporation We agreed that I would start work on May 7, 1973.

During my career with Rockwell International I was promoted several times and retired as Director, Communications Services on November 1, 1992. There were many highlights in my career but two stand out:

- During the initial roll-out of the first Rockwell B-1B bomber aircraft Rockwell sent me in a company plane to Monterey, California to pick up General Jimmy Doolittle and his wife and fly them to Palmdale, California as special guests.
- I was assigned the task of coordinating the Rockwell Guest Viewing Program during the first four flights of the Rock-

well-built Space Shuttle. The vehicles were launched from the Kennedy Space Center in Florida. They landed at Edwards Air Force base in California. NASA allocated Rockwell 600 guests at each location.

A very special Thank You to Harlan Rector, Rom Kimler, and Jack Laffin for allowing me and my family to enjoy a wonderful career all because of The Telephone Call. They saw something in me, and it made all the difference in my life. To them it was a simple phone call, one of maybe dozens they'd make during any given day. To me, it meant a new career, one that got me out of a rut and gave me new challenges and new adventures.

Harvey Alan Hofmann was born in St. Clair Shores, Michigan, on March 7, 1929. He is the eldest of nine children of Arthur and Winifred Hofmann.

Helen Dunn, his first wife of 58 years, died in 2007. The couple had three children: Robert, Anne, and Deborah. Harvey married Susanne Stening in 2009. He lives in Newmarket, UK.

He attended General Motors Institute in Flint, Michigan. In 1948, he enlisted in the U.S. Air Force and graduated with honors as an aerial photographer from the USAF Photo School in Denver, Colorado. He also attended Denver University, the Detroit Institute of Technology, Wayne State University, and the University of Toledo, Ohio.

During the summers of 1949 and 1950, he photomapped the state of Alaska as an aerial photographer crew member on an RB-29. Transferred to Puerto Rico in 1951, he was assigned to a Boeing RB-29 aircraft to photomap the USA Eastern Missile Tracking Range Stations located on islands in the Caribbean Sea. These Stations tracked all manned and unmanned space flights from the Kennedy Space Center in Florida. In 1952, he was honorably discharged as a Staff Sergeant from the USAF after four years of service.

In 1951, the Hudson Motor Car Company in Detroit received a USAF contract to manufacture the USAF Boeing B-47 eight-foot-long nose section and the Boeing RB-47 ten-foot nose section. Upon joining Hudson's in 1952, he was appointed a general foreman on the final installation line for both aircraft nose sections. The USAF cancelled the contract in late 1953.

Harvey joined Abrams Aerial Survey Company in Lansing, Michigan as a photo lab technician. After one year he returned to Detroit to join Teledyne, CAE, a subsidiary of Teledyne, Inc. (formerly Continental Aviation and Engineering Corporation) as a stress lab technician. He became a technical writer, Chief of Technical Publications, and Technical Communications Manager. He resigned after 19 years to join Rockwell International Corporation headquarters in Pittsburgh, Pennsylvania as the Corporate Identity Manager in May 1973.

In 1987, he was transferred to Rockwell's new World Headquarters in El Segundo, California. His responsibilities as Director of Communications Services for Rockwell included Annual Stockholder and Management meetings, and participation in the Paris and Farnborough Air Shows with hospitality chalets, major company exhibits, and company golf events.

Upon his retirement from Rockwell in 1992, he moved to Denver, Colorado, to live near his daughter Anne, her husband Kevin Lillehei and only grandchild Kira. Harvey's outdoor interests were camping, sailing, ice boating and golf.

Notes for your memories of this age:

I MATTER

CHAPTER 5

The Age of Sharing: Family / Marriage / Children

Creativity Matters
By Harlan Rector

In December 2003, caught up in hearing all the Christmas music everywhere, I remembered what a friend said a few years before, "I wonder who that stranger was that took the last room at the Inn in Bethlehem?" When I think too much, sometimes at 3 in the morning, I usually end up acting on my thoughts. Such was the case that night in December.

I started writing the lyrics to a song titled "The Stranger". I didn't know the first thing about writing song lyrics, but when I was finished, I started thinking about other people who might have known Jesus during his three-year ministry on earth. I started writing lyrics to a song Barabbas might sing remembering he was a free man because Jesus was crucified in his place. Then, what about the kid who had a basket of a few fish and two loaves of barley bread? And on and on.

I took a yellow pad with me everywhere I went. I wrote every word on the pad and then I'd two-finger type them on my computer. Never once came the thought of using a rhyming dictionary, the words would tumble out of my mind on to the yellow pad. Spooky as it may sound, I had no idea why I was doing this or where these words were coming from. I was on a mission, and, though I was pretty sure God was somehow behind all this, I didn't want to ask any questions.

When I had about fourteen song lyrics written, without one note of music, I bought an $1,800 keyboard thinking, "If God can have me write lyrics, surely He can help me write the music." Every time I put up a lyric sheet on the keyboard, the melody of a song I already knew would come out of the keyboard. Whenever I feel that God is leading me somewhere, I ask Him to put the right people in my path at the right time. The phone rang and a voice said there was an auction coming up to help pay enormous hospital bills for friends of mine whose daughter was severely handicapped with epileptic seizures. "Was there anything I could contribute for the auction?" One barely used $1,800 keyboard coming up.

Again, the phone rang. Frank, a producer friend in New York, happened to call just to chat.

"What are you doing in St. Louis since you left us?"

"Funny thing you asked," I said, "I've written the lyrics to fourteen songs that I'm thinking could be part of a stage musical, but I don't have one note of music."

"What kind of songs," he asked.

"Well, they're sung by biblical characters about how they knew Jesus."

My friend said, "You should send your lyrics to a guy I know in Nashville, he used to compose show music for me when he lived in New York."

I told Frank that I'd send them to him and if he thought his Nashville friend would be interested, he could suggest my lyrics. Frank got my package and didn't even look at it; he just sent it to Nashville. A couple of week later, this guy I'll call Tony, called to say he loved my lyrics and wanted to write all the music. A door closes, and another one opens.

"Tony" was born and raised a New York Italian. He was a child prodigy, his gift was music. While Tony was creating music to bring the lyrics to bloom, I started writing the "book" or story for a full-blown stage musical. I had no idea what I was doing but I did it. In Tony's studio in Nashville one day, we were having a hard time with some songs. I was so far over my head when it came to composing a song and Tony was losing his patience. We were yelling at each other and I started crying like a baby. Tony didn't know what to think so he asked what was wrong. I sobbed, "I don't know why I am doing this. There are thousands, hundreds of thousands of good writers, why does God want me to do this?" No one had an answer so we kept on working.

Sometime later, the answer came. God doesn't use, and never has, perfect people because there aren't any. He uses sinners because they probably need His attention the most. I used to be put off by the word "sinners". Criticism in today's news relies on a rating system when it comes to sin, but we weren't given the job of judging one sin over the other. Knowing that we're all in this thing together gives me the courage to plow ahead.

I finished writing the "book". The stage musical's title was *A.D.*, since most of the songs were a musical story of Jesus's three-year ministry. To get more songs made and prepare the show for production, I had to get financial help. I invited 40 members of my golf club to a wine and cheese presentation of the musical to come. Eight men showed up and no one was interested. There's that closed door again. Then one of the men, a friend I'll call Tom, buttonholed ten other guys, formed an LLC and raised $24,000 as an investment to get the pre-production done for *A.D.: The Musical.*

In 2010, the Stained Glass Theatre outside of Branson, Missouri liked the music and the story I sent them and said they wanted to run *A.D.* for 18 performances. A three hour and 15 minute drive from St. Louis, I drove down for every rehearsal and every performance. We had three shows every weekend for six weeks, with sold-out audiences at almost all performances. That was seven years after I started writing lyrics. Two years later, the Ivory Theatre in St. Louis ran *A.D.* for ten performances.

Writing is rewriting, so the saying goes. I dropped some songs, wrote some new ones, added new characters and situations, and gave the new show a different title. *A Taste of Heaven* had a very successful stage reading in St. Louis, but we moved to Florida before I could take the show any further. It's very difficult to line up theatres, mostly because theatres run tried and true shows like *Hello Dolly, Oklahoma, Guys and Dolls*, etc. My goal is to see *A Taste of Heaven* as a feature film.

A high school friend's daughter, I'll call her Lisa, in St. Louis, was on cloud nine planning her own daughter's wedding until an accident took the life of the groom-to-be. It was tragic, of course, but the mother-in-law-to-be, our friend's daughter, withdrew and became bitter and in a deep depression, affecting the whole family. It was as if God had taken away Lisa's joy for no reason. After a long period, God's timing is impeccable, *A.D.: The Musical* was playing at the Ivory Theatre and her family wanted to see the show. Lisa reluctantly came as well. One of the things that resonates so well in the songs is how Jesus's Love changed lives. Lisa came out of the theatre, changed. She wrote a thank you note, the only one I ever received, for creating *A.D.: The Musical.*

If only one life is saved, that's all that matters.

ℰℭ

Miracles in a Doctor's Daughter's Life
By Emily Melendez

In February of 1980 my 83-year-old father contracted pneumonia. He had been living with us since June 1979 following his retirement from medical practice. Dr. Sachs was a doctor for 60 years. My husband, my father and I bought a summer house in Greenwood Lake, New York in 1978 with the intention of "winterizing" it for year-round use. "It has so much potential," were the words I used that came back to haunt me. Our plumber had to drill through rock to connect us with village water for winter use. We had a heating system installed and put in a wood-burning stove. Eventually we had to put in a new septic tank as the one we were using was under the house in the "basement".

One morning my dad woke up and as he went to use the bathroom I saw he looked gray and I called for an ambulance. They came but Papa refused to go to the local hospital; he insisted on going to Mother Cabrini Hospital in Manhattan where his friend and colleague worked. So the ambulance drove him down to New York City and when we got there Dr. Gelfand met us. "Your dad has pneumonia," he said and looked at me reproachfully as if it was my fault! I sent the word out to our church and friends: "Pray for my dad!" and pray they did. Papa survived by the grace of God but there was damage to his heart; he had congestive heart failure and would be on five pills daily to avoid fluid build-up in his lungs.

I visited Papa in the hospital and while traveling home by bus I met a very kind lady who was a believer in Christ. We got to conversing and I told her about Papa and about the fact that we hoped to start a family. "We have been trying since September but to no avail," I bemoaned. She replied, "Take B complex and have your husband take zinc." I listened to her advice but by June there were still no signs of a baby in our future. I went on a ladies' retreat to Keswick, New Jersey and one of the speakers was talking about the joys of motherhood and sang, "Turn Around". I started crying quietly and I distinctly heard the

Lord speak to my heart: "Am I not better to you than ten sons?" I answered, "Yes, Lord, you are!" and as I went back to our room I rejoiced that God had spoken to me and met me at my point of need. Excitedly I told my roommate, "The Lord spoke to me!" and Linda looked perplexed as did the other ladies.

"God spoke to me!" I greeted my husband Hannibal with these words and told him what had transpired; he was moved by the words but didn't know what this would mean for us. I found the exact words I heard in the first book of Samuel; Hannah was provoked to tears by Elkanah's other wife, Peninah, because of Hannah's inability to conceive. Elkanah said, "Am I not better to you than ten sons?" After this Hannah prayed to the Lord for a son and promised she would give him back to the Lord if he answered her prayer. He did and she conceived Samuel.

Unbeknownst to me, changes were taking place in my body and I discovered I was pregnant a few weeks later! When I told Hannibal, he said, "You're lying!" That was unexpected! I found out that he had been told he couldn't sire children because of a sickness he contracted as a teen. I assured him I was and his feet didn't touch the ground for nine months! God had performed a miracle and our first daughter was born eight months later. We named her Sarah, "God's princess." Almost five years later, God gave us another gift: our second daughter, Julie Ann. Miracles in our lives! I matter to God and you do, too.

 *Emily Melendez was born in New Orleans, Louisiana and raised in Queens, New York. Her father was a doctor who immigrated to the U.S. when he saw the rise of Nazism in Germany in 1932. He met her mom in Greece after the war while serving in the Army Corps of Engineers.*

Emily graduated from Hobart and William Smith Colleges with an English degree, and earned her teaching credentials from Hunter College in New York and her Master's degree in teaching from SUNY at New Paltz, New York.

Emily taught for 32 years as a reading teacher and elementary school teacher. She and her husband have two daughters, a son-in-law and a 16-year-old grandson. Emily has an identical twin sister and a brother. She has written poetry and journal entries for many years.

❧

The Hitchhikers
By Diane Machaby

On my way home from work at Habitat for Humanity in St. Augustine, Florida on November 12, 2007, I noticed a middle-aged woman, a young man and three small dogs making their way along the interstate. I knew they must be homeless, or trying to make their way back home, as they were laden down with a backpack and small piece of luggage.

I said to myself, "God, if they're still out there when I get back on the interstate, I might pick them up." They were and I did.

All five piled into the back of my van. My initial thoughts were to drive them ten miles north to the exit near my home. After hearing the 40-year-old mother, Sandy, and her 19-year-old son, Michael, tell of how they came to St. Augustine to start a new life, how that did not occur and how they just wanted to get back home, I felt like I wanted to do what I could to help.

Michael said they had not eaten for two days so I stopped at McDonald's and picked up burgers for them and their three small dogs to eat in the car. The dogs were clean, quiet and appeared to be well-behaved. I decided I would drive them to I-10 so they could head towards I-75 that would take them up into Georgia.

During the 45-minute drive, I listened and thought about their situation. By the time we got to I-10, it was getting dark and cold and I felt I just could not leave them on the side of the road so I put them up in a motel next to a truck stop for the night.

The next morning when I called Michael's cell phone, he told me that although they asked a lot of truckers, they could not get a ride. I told Sandy and Michael that "it just so happened" that I would be heading to Valdosta, Georgia, later that day to attend a family reunion (which only occurred once or twice a year) and that I would give them a ride that far.

They were thrilled that I might be able to get them that much closer to home which was near Nashville, Tennessee, over 650 miles away. When I thought about what was going on at work that day, I realized there was nothing more important than trying to help this family get back home. I called my staff at Habitat for Humanity and informed them of my plans. They were concerned about what I was doing and said they would pray for us.

I also called my pastor and my friends at a Christian radio station I listen to, The Promise, telling them the story of the hitchhikers and asking for travel prayers. Because the station is broadcast on the Internet, we virtually had people all over the world praying for us that day.

I arrived at the motel at 10 a.m. to pick up Sandy, Michael and the three dogs, then headed west on I-10. We talked most of the way and they told me how they ended up in their situation. Sandy said she separated from Michael's father then lost her job. A cousin who lived in St. Augustine had brought her and Michael to Florida thinking they could find jobs and housing and begin a new life there. Things didn't work out the way they had hoped so the mother and son made a decision to head back home on their own.

At times, Sandy would get emotional during her conversations. On more than one occasion, she touched my shoulder and tearfully expressed how much she appreciated what I was doing for them. "You're such an angel," she would say.

As we made our way into southern Georgia around noon, I decided to continue driving north towards Macon. I told Sandy and Michael that I didn't need to be in Valdosta until around dinnertime so I felt I had time to drive them a few hours further north and still get back before dark.

Along the route, we talked a lot about where we were from. At one point I asked what type of industry was in their area and why there was high unemployment. Michael mentioned a few businesses in their town that had closed down and also stated he had worked for the Trane Company.

I asked, "Do you mean Trane Air-Conditioning?" He said, "Yes, I worked there last summer with my Dad." Although I didn't know it at the time, this conversation, and this question in particular, were crucial to what would occur later in the day.

As we drove on, something compelled me to push even harder and try to get up past Atlanta. I was concerned and apprehensive about driving through the city because I had never done so before, especially in rush hour traffic. With Michael giving me good directions, I made it just fine. It was then that I informed Sandy and Michael that I would need to start heading back towards Valdosta.

But where would be the best place to leave them? A rest area? I hadn't seen one in a long while and wasn't sure where the next one would be. A restaurant? A truck stop? A gas station or convenience store? I chose an exit on I-75 just north of Atlanta and stopped at a convenience store that had gas pumps. I filled my tank and went to the restroom, all the while thinking to myself … How was I going to leave them here not knowing where they were going to sleep or how they were going to make it home?

It was then that I decided to put them up in a motel another night hoping that a friend or family member could come down and pick them up the following day.

I came out of the store to find Sandy asking a well-dressed business-man whether he was heading north on I-75 and would he be willing to give them a ride. He was, and offered to take them to Chattanooga.

I gave Sandy and Michael a hug and a little money for their trip home. They gathered their dogs and belongings and piled into the man's back seat. I patted the man, whose name was Dennis, on the back of the shoulder, thanking him and handing him my business card. I asked if he would give me a call and leave a message to let me know how things went. He said he would and then took his business card out and handed it to me. It was at that very instant that the miracle occurred.

Dennis worked for the same company as the boy's father! The Trane Company is what Michael had told me when we were discussing what types of industry were in their area. Come to find out … Dennis knew Michael's father! Although Dennis was an executive with the Trane Company in Chattanooga, he knew Michael's father by name and that he worked in the Nashville warehouse.

Not only did Dennis drive them to Chattanooga but he drove them all the way home to Nashville, over 270 miles out of his way!

Written in support of Alpha Omega Miracle Home, this article appeared in Diane Quick-Machaby's When God Showed Up: Recognizing His Hand in Our Lives Charleston, NC, 2017.

ᔥᔐ

Crete Adventure

By Carol Spargo Pierskalla

Sometimes it seems that the good that comes as a result of an accident makes the whole episode worthwhile.

In February 1977, Bill and I were on the island of Crete in the Greek Islands staying at the Creta Maris Hotel. We had decided to spend the day visiting the ruins at Phaestos, about a two-hour drive across the mountains.

During the drive we observed the women in black garments in the vineyards, working with the grapes. Many Cretans have square dark faces and with the addition of black garments, they were quite plain. I mentioned this to Bill and he agreed with me.

When we arrived at the site, no other tourists were there. Two elderly Greek men selling souvenirs were the only people in the area. The ruins were down a hill and there were paths to follow so we began our descent. The terrain was covered in loose gravel but the paths were more secure. After a few minutes I saw an interesting ruin off the path. I left the designated path, took a few steps and lost my footing. I slid downhill, my right leg straight out in front of me, my left leg folding up under me so that when I came down, all my weight landed on my left ankle which was now bent under me, the sole turned up.

Crack!

"Bill! Bill!" I cried out. "I've broken my leg."

"No, I'm sure it's okay. Maybe you sprained it or something."

"No, it's broken." I was quite sure.

We were down a hill, uneven ground slid from under us. Up above were two old men who spoke Greek only, plus a two-hour drive over the mountain in a rented Fiat. How to get me stabilized where I sat was just the first order of business.

"I'll go up the hill and see if I can get some help." Bill was trying to sound confident but I knew that he, too, was thinking of the old men up above and wondering what in the world they could do.

In about ten minutes, Bill came down the hill with a look of wonderment on his face. "You'll never believe it," he said. "There's a Ger-

man tour bus up there and on it there's an Austrian orthopedic sur-
geon—who speaks English!"

Now there are some who call this coincidence, some who call it
synchronicity, but I call it an answer to prayer.

First, the surgeon came down the hill and showed Bill how to make
a sling with their hands so they could carry me up the hill. When we
reached the top, they deposited me in the car with my legs hanging
out. After examining my leg, the surgeon agreed that it was broken. He
asked the bus driver for the first aid kit and some splints. When the old
men who had been there earlier, realized what was needed, they imme-
diately set off to find something that could be used. They returned with
small pieces of bamboo that made excellent splinting material.

How could I have thought that these lovely old men were just
grubby tourist abusers? They were so concerned for my welfare that
they found just what was needed!

After asking that we bring him copies of the x-rays from the hos-
pital, the surgeon (who also "just happened" to be staying at the Creta
Maris) helped to position me in the back seat of the Fiat and Bill and I
were on our way across the mountain. During the drive, whenever the
pain took over I recited the Lord's Prayer. When the pain receded as it
invariably did, I felt the tears slipping down my cheeks. I was grateful
for the help I received.

Once we were back in Heraklion, we tried to find the hospital.
Even a policeman we asked didn't know! It wasn't until Bill had the
bright idea to ask two older women in black at a cemetery, that we
finally found out where it was!

After trying to communicate with the admissions people in French
and failing miserably, they sent for an x-ray technician who spoke very
good English. Yes, the leg was broken just above the ankle but no doc-
tor could see me until the next morning during his normal rounds. So
I had to stay overnight in the hospital. I don't remember panicking. I
seem to remember feeling quite calm. Probably all that praying!

The hospital ward held about 10 women in various stages of or-
thopedic distress. All of them had caregivers—women family mem-
bers—who were helping. No one spoke English but I had my trusty
little Berlitz book and was able to communicate minimally. I soon dis-
covered that I was a celebrity. The "American turista" was an object

of curiosity to almost everyone in the hospital. One man brought his little son in to see me, patted my hand and my cheek and murmured reassuring words. At least I think that's what they were. I don't really know as they were Greek.

I did find out that "pono" was "pain" as the women caregivers in the room said sympathetically, "Pono? Pono?" as they patted and tut-tutted. They were wonderfully sweet and they made me feel cared for. When the nurse (the only one I saw in 24 hours) came in with a little bottle and tried to tell me what she wanted, I looked under the medical section of my Berlitz book and found, "I need a urine sample." I showed it to her at which point she took the book all around the ward showing everyone what was in there and laughing along with everyone else.

The problems came later. First of all I was in some pain; secondly there was no nursing care as such. Women family members provided the care and the food, except for yogurt, rice and milk. Since I was only equipped with men family members, I was in trouble. They had to leave me there with no one to care for me. No problem! I was adopted! Other women's caregivers washed me, brought me the bed pan and even shared their food with me. It was a humbling experience. I couldn't believe that I had ever thought of these women as plain. They were exceedingly beautiful inside and out!

The next morning the doctor arrived. He managed to hurt everyone he touched by his rough treatment. He did speak English, however. He then proceeded to cast my leg while his assistant held it up by my toes. It was painful but I had a lot of sympathy around me.

When I left the hospital, the families were outside. Bill was driving and said, "There are some folks behind us who want your attention." I turned around in my seat and there were all the women who had helped me. They did not want me to leave before they had a chance to say goodbye!

When one considers the situation: broken leg, the hospital, the lack of nursing care, the shortage of food and the insensitive doctor, it could have been a tragedy. Instead it is one of the most wonderful experiences of my life.

ℰ℧℞

I Am Iron Man
By Hollis Donaldson

I find it humbling that God gives us certain times in our lives that are pivotal, those times end up molding us into the person we are truly meant to be.

If people were to ask "What do you think of Hollis Donaldson? What kind of man is he?" I want their first thoughts to be of my faith and family. Without them I am not who I am. I matter because that combination completes me.

I have been blessed in my life to have parents both from different cultures come together to provide me with a life that allowed me to chase my dream, which in my late teens until early 20s was to play professional soccer. I was blessed to have been drafted for Major League Soccer in 2005 and played for one year with the Chicago Fire.

BUT nothing has come easy in my life. I have always had to grind and work for everything, which in my eyes is good. It teaches you perseverance, humility and a relentlessness that I always relate to my faith. A hunger to succeed, to improve that never ceases.

Ultimately I came to a point in my life where I could have continued to pursue professional soccer or create a stable foundation for the family I was about to build. Family first.

Fast forward 13 years: My wife, Jamie, and I have four kids—Harlow, Honor, Harbor and Hilton—whom we adore. As with all marriages, Jamie and I have to put in the work. When doing so, you end up loving the person you marry even more on an entirely different level. Our family foundation is based on our faith, love, and hard work. No excuses. Our goal is to raise our  kids in today's society to be confident in who they are. To have good character takes work but it's my wife's and my purpose because THEY matter.

At age 33 I had a stroke, unexpectedly. The doctors diagnosed it as a VAD (Vertebral artery dissection). This may from the outside seem negative but it turned into my positive in life. It turned my life and my family's life upside down for almost two years yet we are stronger for it. I had to learn to walk again, and undergo visual and speech therapy. I regained 95% of my normal function back except for some nerves in my leg. With the assistance of my wife, who is an expert (an understatement!) in personal training, and help from our family and church, we made it.

My wife designed my training programs that helped me once again compete with her in Ironman triathlons. It wasn't easy, some days were darker than others, but the main concept I kept telling myself was to keep going. My kids, my family, the purpose in my life—I had to keep going. During the next two years of post-stroke recovery, I was going to work, where I'd put up a false front—a wall—to hold my emotions in check. But when I came home at night, that wall had physically and emotionally worn me down and would hit me like a ton of bricks. My body was still healing itself and I was exhausted. Little things like wrestling with the kids or the normal sounds they make around the house became amplified, and not in a good way. I had nothing left and just needed to sleep so I could function the next day.

My kids would whisper "let's make sure we are quiet so Daddy doesn't have to go to the hospital again." Those comments as a dad don't tear you down. They kept me going. They gave me fuel to be more for them, be more for those around me.

You're not alone in having to work hard. Sometimes just living your daily life takes its toll on you. Everyone wears a mask, and you should know that it's ok and normal to feel exhausted from the weight of that mask.

My wife would tell you I have a tough exterior but truly am just an introvert whose drive to succeed and love for His God and family has no bounds. She tells me all the time I make her a better version of herself but the truth is they do. I guess this is what you want to have in life and what I want for my kids.

Know you have a purpose in life for yourself so that you understand you matter. God created us for a purpose, His purpose. Find love that changes you into a better version of yourself. I have and because of this I wake up humbled every day. I am forever grateful.

Hollis Donaldson was born in Manhattan, New York to Hugo and Karen Donaldson. Karen is African American and Hugo is of Costa Rican descent. He has two other brothers, Haefen and Hugo, and a sister, Andrea. After attending Providence Prep school in Jacksonville, Florida, he earned his Bachelor's degree in International Business and an MBA in Business Administration from Liberty University. #33 played as a defender for the Chicago Fire Major League Soccer team before coming to Jacksonville to begin his career. Hollis and wife Jamie compete in Iron Man triathlons as their outlet to relax. He was recently featured in Triathlete Magazine about his return to the sport post-stroke. When Hollis is not training or watching his kids compete his favorite thing to do is watch movies with his wife and kids or read a good book.

He spent time with CSX Transportation, a Class I freight railroad and leading supplier of rail-based freight transportation in North America. There Hollis was the Director of Operations for the Receivables and Credit teams and served as Chief of Staff to the CFO.

Hollis earlier served as Senior Vice President of Fraud Operations at Citi, where he was responsible for the strategy development and implementation of the Fraud Operations footprint for both domestic and international site locations and directly oversaw performance for all staffed vendor locations in Central America and Asia. He led planning and program management for the Fraud Operations Automation roadmap. Throughout his nearly nine years at Citi, he advanced through management roles of increasing responsibility within the Customer Service and Collections organization and received multiple awards for his distinguished leadership. He was named the 2019 Jacksonville Business Journal 40 Under 40 Honoree.

Hollis joined SoFi as Director of Partnership Operations in August 2020. He manages operations for the Money partnership portfolio and is responsible for strategic operational vision for the Samsung partnership inclusive of service delivery, operational cost management of the portfolio, customer experience and productivity improvement.

ஓ(ᴃ

Looking for Thankfulness
By Jennifer Lewis Keller

I married my college sweetheart, Kent, in 1997. When we met, I was drawn to his calm, soft-spoken nature, and the way he cared for people and made everyone feel valued and important. He treated me as if I were the greatest gift he'd been given, and I honestly think he believed that I was. His love for people, especially those who were hurting and in need of hope, served him well as we left college and he attended seminary to pursue a ministry degree, and then to serve in church ministry. In 2004, God blessed us with our daughter, Kenlee, who was the joy of our lives. Then, in 2007, we were blessed with a second daughter, Chloee. Both were "daddy's girls" to the core. We served three different churches during eight years, some of which were difficult experiences. During the hard times, we would keep a "Thankful List" and would write down things we were thankful for, in order to keep a positive perspective and focus on the good we saw God doing.

In 2008, we moved to Georgia and left church ministry for Kent to work for a financial ministry, helping people who were in desperate life situations due to financial crises of various sorts. This was a very different type of ministry, yet one he greatly enjoyed, and his coworkers quickly became like family to us. He often told me stories of people he "got" to talk to who were suicidal over their money situations, and how he considered it a privilege to share with them that there was hope and that God still had a plan for each of them.

In July 2011, that belief in God's plan was tested. Kent had been experiencing some severe back pain and, despite multiple trips to his doctor, he remained in pain. On Sunday, July 24, while I was out with our daughters, he bent over to pick something up, felt a pop in his back, and fell to the floor in pain. He was unable to get up on his own, not even to let the neighbor in to help him. I drove home as fast as I could and I found him lying in our living room floor, saying he couldn't feel his legs. I helped him get to a sitting position against the sofa and the EMTs soon arrived. I remember thinking, as he was wheeled into the ER, that worse-case scenario, my husband would be paralyzed and in a wheelchair.

I never could have prepared myself for what was coming. After multiple tests and hours of waiting, we were told that Kent had cancer. Cancer. Multiple metastases, in his lung, kidney, and liver, as well as a mass pushing on his spine. We were immediately transferred from our small-town hospital to a bigger facility in Atlanta. It took nearly two weeks to determine what type of cancer we were fighting and what the treatment plan would be. We decided this was a good time to bring the thankful list back, so we started it on that first day of diagnosis. I had always claimed Jeremiah 29:11 as my "life verse":

"For I know the plans I have for you, declares the Lord, plans to prosper you and not to harm you, to give you a future and a hope."

I clung to that promise during those days, and we continued to write daily in the journal we used for our thankful list (which we referred to as "The List"). There were lots of days that we wrote about the people taking care of us, from doctors and nurses to friends and family who supported us financially and cared for our girls. On the hard days, we made ourselves look for the things to be thankful for: a beautiful sunrise when  we hadn't slept much that night, an anonymous donation to our bank account to help sustain us, a conversation with a stranger that was encouraging. I would often have something happen during the day and think to myself, "That's what I'm putting on The List tonight."

After three months of outpatient chemo that didn't work, Kent and I travelled to several other states seeking other treatments, including a stem cell transplant. Unfortunately, those treatments didn't work, either. Through all of this, we continued to daily write something on The

List, and we continued to be supported by caring people all around us. For Christmas in 2011, a family "adopted" us for the holiday and showered us with more gifts than I'd ever seen! In May, our small-town community and our college friends sent us on an all-expense-paid, ten-day trip to Walt Disney World! That trip held surprise after surprise and gave us an abundance of things for The List. There were also things such as having a "normal" day as a family at home or getting to go to church. Not everything was a huge event; some were everyday activities that we had taken for granted until we didn't have them anymore. Whatever we were feeling thankful for that day made it to The List.

By mid-summer 2012, things didn't look so promising. I remember asking God where the "future and hope" and the "plans to prosper and not harm" were. Then, in August, surrounded by our girls, friends and family, I had the privilege of holding Kent's hand as he slipped from this life into his eternal one in Heaven. I had promised him, though, that we would keep The List, and on that day, I wrote: "Kent is with Jesus. He went surrounded by people who love him."

The girls and I continued adding to The List every day. Some days were harder than others. But I also went back to Jeremiah and did some more reading. I had stopped at verse 11, because I loved the idea of a prosperous future. But verses 12-14 give a little more instruction:

"'Then you will call on me and come and pray to me, and I will listen to you. You will seek me and find me when you seek me with all your heart. I will be found by you,' declares the Lord, 'and will bring you back from captivity.'"

What I didn't realize, was that in writing something on The List every day, I was learning a different perspective. I believe that there is good in every single day. There is something that God is doing, and something to be thankful for. Most of the time, we're too busy to see it. But if we make a point to look for it, we'll see it. Eventually, it becomes easy to be thankful, and that thankfulness becomes our character.

A year after Kent died, I met a wonderful man named Stephen (who had lost his wife to cancer). We married a year after that, and in another year had a son, Paxton. Through all of it, we have continued to keep The List as a family, looking for the things in each day to be thankful for. Perhaps that's a job promotion, or perhaps it's something as simple as a day with a  friend or an hour of quiet at the beach. We keep looking for the thankfulness, and, sure enough, we keep finding it.

Jennifer Lewis Keller lives in Florida, but is a Tennessee girl at heart. She loves the mountains, photography, writing about life, time with her family, and a good cup of sweet tea. She's been an elementary school teacher, a minister's wife, and a full-time mom. She teaches preschool, serves in her church, and hopes to start a non-profit. She is the wife of Stephen, and mom to her three greatest accomplishments: Kenlee, Chloee and Paxton.

ℰℭ

Opposites Matter
By Chuck Brockmeyer

Way back in 1975 I married a beautiful girl named Patricia. I had never thought about marriage prior to the light bulb turning on in my head and me saying to myself, "Gee, I think I should marry Pat." Then answering myself, "OK, I'll give it a chance."

Long haired, self-centered, a Studio Art major in college, I thought of myself as an artist, but did little consistent work to prove it. Now this was the post-hippie, free love era and people were settling down into a more realistic lifestyle.

She was so solid, she took no crap, was self-giving and quietly strong, I never knew a person so even-keeled, dependable, with so much common sense. In contrast I was careless, self-absorbed, undisciplined, and flighty—all the things promoted in the seventies. When I finally married Pat it was like the words of Dave Barry the humorist, "Men are like grapes and women like wine presses. It takes a good woman to smash the heck out of you and make you into something presentable to have at the dinner table."

She was so inspiring to me that, after proving her worth time and time again, I had to admit my missteps and to start taking her advice and promptings seriously. This was the key to success; as she always reminds me, "happy wife happy life".

Now being retired I have also found out living together for all the hours of every day she intuitively knows the right decision. Boy, I have to pull the mustard with her, but hey, we are successful, and have a great partnership.

We both like to travel, have adventures, and love nature. I am directionally challenged and she is so good with directions. I even call her Scout. She can even tell the direction by the time of day and the sun. We both like projects, remodeling, yard work, a good movie and our two beautiful girls.

Growing old together with my wife is what I look forward to. I know that God will bless our love.

❧❧❧

How To Pick Up...Your Life
By Ed Mickolus

Many couples have "meet cute" stories. Here's ours, with an epilogue.

In Washington, D.C., many professionals have 60 hours/week jobs, and simply don't have time to devote to the more traditional ways of meeting potential partners—through friends, at restaurants/ watering holes, through blind dates, through clubs catering to common interests (once you're home, you're tired, you have time to feed your pets and yourself, then you just want to turn in). The Open University,

First Class, and other informal adult education groups hosted classes that offered opportunities to meet people. Among others, I took "How to Write/Answer In Search Of Ads" (these ISO ads were very popular among Washington yuppies in the 1980s), "Chutzpah 101" (getting things done more efficiently in social situations), and "How to Pick Up Quality Women—For Men Only" (a similarly-titled "How to Pick Up Quality Men—For Women Only" was also available, apparently with many of the same insights). Homework for the latter courses was to attend a get-together, hosted by one of the instructors who taught cooking courses, of ten male and ten female alumni of the courses, with the same age/socioeconomic status.

I wasn't feeling especially well that evening, but something told me that this would be an opportunity like no other. So I toughed out the long drive and queasy stomach, and made it to the party, somewhat intimidated by the collection of Ferraris and Mercedes that lined the driveway.

Guaranteed to have something in common to talk about, the attendees didn't have to worry about using standard icebreakers, or even employ the tips learned in class. Folks just dove right into conversations, knowing that they were at the party for the same reason.

I met numerous (well, ok, ten, final offer) women, but Susan clearly stood out. We had a lot in common. Her job was similar to mine—she was a researcher for the Library of Congress, which required her to pore through reams of data each day, quickly writing reports for demanding clients who were voracious readers. (I was an analyst at the Central Intelligence Agency—the jobs were comparable, although I had to dig through classified materials as well.). We drove the same model car, lived with two cats, even used the same brand of vacuum cleaner. Did I mention that she was beautiful and for reasons unclear to me, laughed at my humor? I couldn't wait for July 2 to arrive—it was to be our first date. We went to one of DC's discos; she was the best dance partner I've ever had, with a gentle yet electric touch and instinctive feel for hand signaling. She was also a fascinating conversationalist. That night, I sat my cats down and let them know that two other cats, and their owner, would be joining our lives.

On our second date, we shared our patriotism, walking from the Pentagon parking lot to the National Mall, where we sat under the shadow of the Washington Monument to listen to the traditional Beach Boys concert and take in the July 4 fireworks. Future dates entailed much more dining, dancing, and fireworks.

Great meeting, great first date, great second date, great 17th date. We met on June 23, she said "Yes" on October 17 (sending helium-filled balloons with "Yes" on them to my Agency office—the Office of Security called me to the front desk to sign for them), we were married on January 15 (would have been sooner, but there was an IRS "marriage penalty" back then—scheduling around the penalty essentially paid for the wedding). We still celebrate each of those important dates.

We've enjoyed being married to each other so much that we renewed our vows on our 27th anniversary at our local parish.

Our attending Mass together every Sunday led her to choose to be baptized and confirmed as a Catholic shortly after we retired and moved to Florida, living a few hours from our beloved daughter. One of the reasons we chose our area was a sermon given by a charismatic priest, who said, "You should turn to your spouse each day and acknowledge that you are each other's blessing." That struck a chord with us, and ever since, our first words to each other every morning are "Good morning, Blessing."

God clearly intended for us to be together. I'm so glad I listened when He said, "Go to the party. It'll change your life."

Notes for your memories of this age:

I MATTER

CHAPTER 6

The Age of Reflection: Retirement

ॐQR

Finding Meaning in "Retired" Life
By Ed Mickolus

My professional career let me make a difference, and sometimes, history. I was an analyst, operations officer, and manager with the Central Intelligence Agency, battling terrorists, drug traffickers, proliferators of chemical, biological, nuclear, and radiological weapons, rogue regimes, and various other no-goodniks. Sometimes, we'd save the world before breakfast! One a quieter day, before lunch. I worked with incredibly dedicated colleagues, motivated by a well-articulated mission of providing the best intelligence to policymakers to make informed decisions. We were on the side of the Good Guys, protecting our fellow Americans, serving as the tip of the spear, ensuring against disasters.

Such careers rarely gave us time to raise the question: "What next?" When you're in the greatest job one can ever have, there is no second choice on the list. Many of us had 30-, 40-, even 50- year careers in intelligence. Some of my friends devoted 60 years to US intelligence, with careers that predated the formation of CIA.

But most of us retire before six decades, and are suddenly faced with our own "What Next?" With advances in medical science, healthy lifestyles, and a Type A approach to life, many of us have another 30 years to go before, well, you know. So what can we do in our remaining time that is anywhere near as fulfilling?

It's unlikely that one is going to find a second option that will give the opportunity to make a difference on such a grand scale as we at the Agency had in our globetrotting jobs. But that doesn't mean that one can't contribute on a smaller scale, drawing upon the talents that one developed before retirement, either professionally or via hobbies.

Looking for ventures, or creating one's own, that offer the chance to continue serving others, was key for me. I've always been taken by the Parable of the Talents, in which we are called upon to serve the

Lord with what we are given. Keep trying until you're called back to Heaven, don't just rest on your laurels. To do so, I've looked at what I have to offer irrespective of my job, and have pursued:

- Teaching what I know at the University of North Florida's franchise of the Osher Lifelong Learning Institute (OLLI), giving participants a feeling for what it is that intelligence officers do for our country. I also offer courses in creativity and writing.

- Using my (so I'm told—listenable) voice as an announcer for a number of organizations, including anchoring our community's dance travel team that performs at assisted living facilities, emceeing performances of our community's theater group, hosting trivia games, and lectoring (reading the Epistles during Mass) at our church.

- Serving as a newsreader to the blind for WJCT-FM, the local NPR affiliate. Hundreds of blind and vision-impaired listeners tune in to the radio station to hear volunteers read the local newspaper to them.

- Acting as a "standardized patient" at Jacksonville University's Brooks Rehabilitation College of Healthcare Sciences, working with students in the speech pathology, nursing, and counseling departments to give them a more realistic experience of dealing with patients than would be the case by simply roleplaying to each other.

- Continuing to write books on my professional specialties — terrorism, education, and intelligence. While I'm no longer personally chasing terrorists, I can still help those who hope to become a counterterrorist professional, or those who have landed such positions.

All of these activities give me the impression that I still have something to offer to various generations, not just fellow Boomers, and that I can still be relevant, no matter what society thinks of my rapidly advancing age.

Many of my colleagues have had similar experiences in "giving back". (I've never been a fan of "it's now time to give back". That's what our CIA careers were all about—serving our fellow citizens. We're just continuing our service, in a different guise.) One need not settle into being put on the shelf after one's first career. There are always opportunities out there to continue to matter.

℘Q

Everyone Retires, Not Always Contented
By Harlan Rector

In Chapter 4, I wrote about spending my lunch hour drawing caricatures of celebrity guests on a radio interview show in 1971 and 1972. It's all a blur as far as my memory is concerned. I don't remember anything about my job at the ad agency during that time and I honestly can't remember one word that was ever spoken by any of the 100-plus celebrities that I "lunched" with. Catching an expression and drawing a likeness were all that was on my mind. It was the closest out-of-body and mind experience I will ever have.

I was blessed with the gift of art and took it for granted. The things that matter in one's life must be backed up with character or they are just irresponsible fluff.

Things changed in late 1972. My detractor at the ad agency left, I was promoted and with my new responsibility, I had to give up my lunch gig at WJR radio. I was given more responsibility and traveled all over the country for location shooting. One year I made fifteen trips to LA, each for a week or more. When I asked to be transferred to the LA office they said no and gave me more creative responsibility, an enormous project for a new client, Goodyear. I decided to quit and move my family as soon as the Goodyear project was over. I did, and in the summer of 1975, my wife and I and five kids headed to LA in a station wagon and a U-Haul truck.

The family was happy but the next seven years was a revolving door of career moves. Three different ad agencies, one of my own, a film production company and freelance art jobs didn't offer much of a future for me or my family.

But God wasn't through with me.

I was given the gift of voice, but not until 1980 was I actually discovered, by the top voiceover woman in LA, to have a voice talent for TV and radio commercials. Gratified and bewildered by this gift, I prayed for God to take control of this new career and it altered my life on the outside, though I doubt if anyone noticed since I did such a good job with character fluff.

After a year of voiceovers in LA we moved to Connecticut and I commuted to New York for the next 20 years as my new career flourished. We found a small church in Connecticut that was packed with a large spirit of God in its people. I was encouraged to attend a three-day men's retreat called Tres Dias. My wife would attend a retreat for women two weeks later. There were as many men on the team that conducted the Tres Dias weekend as there were men who attended.

At a lunch break on the second day, a few of us were throwing a football back and forth, I reached for a pass and heard and felt a snap. The pulled hamstring was so painful I collapsed. Two guys helped me back to the meeting. The "Rector" of the team started the afternoon with his presentation and then stopped, saying, "A brother is hurting, and when we know someone is hurting we should pray for him. So let's go lay hands on Harlan and pray for his comfort and healing."

Almost 50 men came to where I was sitting and began praying for me. I "felt" the weight of 50 hands and started crying. I had never felt such overwhelming love before. The pain in my leg was gone. I was touched by God. Later, I remember thinking about all the ways Jesus revealed God's love for His people, especially when He gave us a path to forgiveness. The last part of forgiving the woman about to be stoned for adultery was often ignored by me. Jesus said, "I don't condemn you. You are forgiven, now go and sin no more." I changed on the inside.

This essay is in Chapter 6 because I retired from my old self long ago. Since then, God has given me opportunities to use my creativity for His Glory. Now, at age 86, I can't wait for the next time I'll step out fearlessly knowing I matter to my God.

℘ℂ

Walking in the Shoes
of the Homeless
By Tracy Tripp

I began my writing journey about eight years ago. That's when I became serious about it, anyway. In each of my stories, I thrust the protagonist into a situation that can either lead to destruction or makes them stronger. Why? Well, I suppose it is because of my relationship with life and how I view it. We are all living a story, and the great narrator is constantly thrusting his characters into situations that I believe are always intended to make them stronger. As a writer, I delve into human emotions, fears, strengths, and weaknesses that make us survivors or victims. The outcome often depends on ourselves, but that is not to discount the helping hands that reach out to us on our journey.

Perhaps it is my love of stories and the impact that life has on each of us that I became empathetic to the homeless people's plights on the streets of Jacksonville. I wanted to understand and give them a chance to help others understand that sometimes we drown under the pressure life puts on us. Sometimes, despite the helping hands reaching out, the swim to the surface simply feels too difficult.

I began my journey with a friend, Dorri, and Dale, a connection that I made through some contacts on Facebook. Dale lovingly refers to the homeless people in Jacksonville as his "street friends". His help is priceless

Dorri and Tracy: Two friends on a journey
to make a difference

because he can select suitable candidates for us to speak to—meaning we will be safe, and they will be able to understand the waiver they sign.

On our first day, we spoke with two people whose parents abandoned them—one as an infant on a doorstep and one as a five-year-old in a train station. Another young man suffered from abuse and was struggling to feel normal again. Two of the men worked for much of their lives, but due to becoming disabled on the job, they could no longer earn an income. One sweet man watched all his earnings slip away, unable to stop the bleed before losing his house.

We drove home the first day in silence. It seemed our drives home were often quiet as we tried to digest everything we had heard. It wasn't only their stories that weighed on us, but everything behind their stories. The problems appeared insurmountable. The first problem is the lack of good parenting. Grand ideas came to my mind, ideas that I must admit will most likely never be realized.

I remember one day, after several interviews, I was sitting by my pool watching the birds on my birdfeeder and the deer running back and forth as they do most mornings. I sipped my coffee and took my quiet time to be thankful for my blessings. Mornings are a treasured time for me. The peacefulness helps me prepare for the day to come. When stressful situations come up, I remember those quiet memories and respond to issues with calmness.

My mind experienced one of those moments when I refused to see obstacles. I dreamed of founding a place where parents could go to capture some of the calm I get to experience. After all, don't we all deserve that simple pleasure? I envisioned a home on the water where parents could come when they feared they would hurt their child— parents whose only training came from a previous generation of struggling parents. My imaginary refuge had meditation rooms, parenting classes, gardens, and crafts. As parents developed their inner peace, their child/children would also see counselors and receive positive reinforcement. They would experience loving discipline, and then we would bring the parents and children together and practice interacting appropriately. But reality is reality, and I have no idea how to create the refuge that exists only in my mind.

The other problem that weighed on us was the hopelessness. There is a huge catch 22 for people on the streets. Even if they beat their drug problems or alcohol addictions, they need a job to afford a home. How does one interview for a job when they don't have clean clothes and can't shower? There are fantastic services such as Love Cleans that offer showers at least once a week, but who can be outside in the Florida air for days on end and then go in to work? Daily showers are a necessity for someone to look and feel professional.

Despite that problem, even if they land a job, their income would be too meager to afford a home. Affordable housing—we heard the complaint repeatedly. No one wants affordable housing built in their vicinity, but if the development is too far away, they won't have access to public transportation and other services.

The problems made me feel small and incapable. How was one addicted to drugs and alcohol going to kick habits that celebrities who appear to have access to the best facilities and unlimited money cannot defeat? How can they envision a life they never witnessed, full of love and stability?

But possibly the story that got to me the most, the one that kept me up at night just a bit longer, was quite different than the ones above. The story that put fear in my bones is the one that brought those problems to my very doorstep.

One sweet woman shared her story with us while she was in rehab. It did not involve abuse, addictive parents, abandonment, or poverty. This woman began her life in a lovely home with loving parents. But she also had a draw for the excitement that usually came in the form of the "bad boy" type. She began drinking and hanging out with young men who encouraged dangerous behavior. After an abortion, one such person offered her drugs, and her life spiraled. After several abusive relationships, she found herself eating out of garbage cans and living on the streets at the age of fifty. Her parents asked her what they could have done to change how things ended up, and she answered honestly, "Nothing."

I'm a parent of three children in high school and college. We are not strangers to the temptations that they face. We try our best to have a close relationship with each one where they know they can come to us. But her word, "Nothing", is terrifying. Each time I send my kids out into the world, I pray that they never try drugs—not even once. For some, that's all it took. With that one decision, the world we sometimes try to avoid eye contact with can come banging on our door. And maybe to my surprise, that is what I learned most by interviewing our "street friends". I thought I would be telling others to remember that we are all not that different, but I was surprised to find their stories opened my eyes as well.

Authors like to write endings that are wrapped up nicely and, ideally, happy. When I interviewed many of these people, I wondered, will their story have a happy ending? And if not, was there something we could have done? I refuse to believe, as we all should, that the answer to that question is "Nothing."

ഇാൔ

Memories of Theo
By Chuck Brockmeyer

Just a quick background of my grandmother Theo:

I never met any of my natural grandmothers or grandfathers as they were gone before my birth. But, my grandfather had married a second time after his first wife died and this step grandmother was all grandparents wrapped into one as far as my sister and me were concerned. She was a special independent woman whom I loved very much.

She was the seventh child, along with three other daughters and three brothers, of a Lutheran Pastor in Albert Lee, Minnesota. She was always proud of her name and repeated it to us many times: Theodora Sophia Elizabeth Smeby Burmiester. Each name had a special meaning but was lost to me during the passing of all the years although I heard the other children envied her for her father naming her Theodora, which meant "Blessed by God".

She developed a reputation in town of being a courageous adventurist. Still living with the family, she and her sister decided to attempt a road trip all the way to New York City in an old Model T Ford. In the early 1900s, roads were not very reliable so they strung up nine spare tires to the back end of the car for the trip. They packed up all their suitcases and got ready to go. The word spread around town about the planned adventure and soon the local newspaper showed up at their door and asked to interview them. They became local superstars for attempting their risky road trip.

Theo was tall and athletic; she played, then coached, basketball. She also was an avid golfer right into her senior years. There were many stories of her exploits. One story was of her sitting in the stands of a poorly refereed basketball game. She became boisterous at the ref's lousy calls to the point where the frustrated fellow said, "Well if you think you can do any better you can just come out here and do it yourself!" She stood up, came down the stands, grabbed his whistle, and finished the game to the cheers of the audience.

Here is the story I would like to give you, as it was a remarkable and emotional event that took place around my grandmother's passing. I came upon it recently while reading through some of my old journal entries of notable happenings in my life:

I always have had fond memories of my grandmother Theo. When I was 13 she brought me out West to see relatives who lived in Chinook, Washington. We traveled by Great Northern Vista Viewer train, which was great for me, especially the top deck with the solarium windows. Our trip took us through Glacier National Park. I remember the view as being spectacular.

When I was young I would come to spend a few days with her in Mankato, Minnesota. It was just my grandmother and me because I had her all to myself. We would take walks downtown to shop and talk then finally end up at Woolworths for an ice-cream sundae.

She always carried herself elegantly. Her tall stature and nicely groomed features always impressed on me that my grandmother was someone special.

Many years later, I was married with three children and my grandmother was living at a nursing home in Albert Lea, Minnesota. She was very old and had been losing ground mentally and physically after a series of strokes. She also had broken her hip, which put her in a wheelchair. At 93 years of age, we all wondered how long she would be with us.

My young family hadn't seen my grandmother in a while and I began thinking of going to see her soon. In fact, that night after falling asleep, I had an unusual dream about her:

There I was, anxiously waiting outside my grandmother's old grey house intending to do some sort of maintenance work. I was locked out with my grandmother nowhere in sight. The unsettling thought came to me of her getting lost or falling down somewhere with no one to help. I was angry with myself for not driving her here from the nursing home myself. Of course, in reality she hadn't lived in the grey house for over 15 years.

As I stood there fretting and pacing I turned to see a tall stately woman walking down the sidewalk in front of the old grey house. Her appearance caught my eye because she seemed so radiant. She was an older lady, but then again not, for she had a healthy, ageless look about her.

She seemed to sense my distress and walked over to me on the lawn. As she looked into my eyes, I was struck at how her features were so alive and glowing. Her beautiful silver hair shone in the sunlight. Darker streaks of silver were running attractively though it.

Did I know her? Her eyes looked familiar, very clear and intelligent with a look that seemed to say, "Why are you in such a state, could there be anything in this world to cause you so much worry?"

As I tried to explain to the woman why I was upset, I turned towards the old grey house and stopped in mid-sentence. There in the picture window was my aged grandmother. She was moving about, all stooped over with her hair disheveled, just like the way I remembered her looking the last time I had visited the nursing home.

Her shadowy figure in the picture window caused a pain of remorse that overwhelmed me. To see her in that condition was such a contrast to my childhood memories of my grandmother.

"There she is now," I remarked. "I had better go and help her..." I started to say to the lady on the walk, but to my surprise she had disappeared! Wait! Now I finally recognized who the radiant lady on the front walk was and why she looked so familiar, it was my grandmother! But how could it be? I turned and looked for the old figure of my grandmother in the picture window, but it too was gone. I immediately woke up.

I usually don't remember my dreams but this one was so real and had such an emotional impact on me that I wondered what it all meant.

I was busy at work the next day when I received a call from my parents telling me that Theo had passed away the night before.

Was God trying to prepare me for my grandmother's death so the shock of it wouldn't hit me so hard? It all started to make sense to me. The old mental picture I had of my grandmother in the nursing home—confused, enfeebled, deteriorating—was replaced with a picture of her in a new heavenly state, full of life, ageless and happy. She was with Jesus now. There is no need for me to feel bad or hopeless.

I found out first-hand that God does make all things better for those who believe. We can trust in Him for our future, in fact, what a confidence He gives us for facing the troubles and pains of each day!

ℰ) Cℛ

The End: Making a Difference After You've Gone
By Ed Mickolus

One last try, and it worked.

When we look back on our lives, we're left with wondering if we had a life well lived. In the limited amount of time we have left, what else can we do to justify our having been here? Did we make a difference? Did we help others? Is the world a better place for us having been here?

Whatever you decide to answer to fill your final days on earth, there's one last gift you can make that will outlive your time here.

Organ donation to a hospital can save eight lives and enhance more than 100 lives via tissue grafts. Donating your body to science for medical school research and instruction in anatomy is crucial in advancing knowledge and preparing the next generation of medical professionals. You can also donate to "body farms" in the U.S., Canada, and Australia that help budding forensic anthropologists and crime science investigators learn about body decomposition in various environments and train cadaver dogs. So even when you're gone, you're still contributing to the betterment of the world.

My donation also let me check off a "bucket list" item of my parents. Having grown up in Lawrence, Massachusetts, just a few miles away from Cambridge, they'd always envisioned their only child going to Harvard, and even sent me to Phillips Academy in Andover — essentially, Harvard Prep — for a short stint. But when I applied to undergrad and grad schools, Harvard's undergrad school, grad school, law school, and Kennedy School wished me well elsewhere. (Elsewhere became Georgetown for undergrad and Yale for my doctorate.) Harvard essentially said "we'll let you in over your dead body." Learning of their medical training program using cadavers, I took them up on the offer, filled out the Medical School's paperwork, and we shook on it. (Right after I got in, so I hear, they changed their admission requirements for scientific donations!) I suspect the Harvard med students will take particular delight in opening up a Yale guy to see what makes us tick. And maybe down the road those students will know what makes you tick, and can save your life.

So if you find me in extremis, just put a stamp on me and mail me to Cambridge. They'll know what to do. And I'll have one final chance to matter.

Notes for your memories of this age:

Epilogue

ℰᎧᏋ

A Salute to Life Savers
By Pat Krause

Lest we become discouraged by the constant barrage of hate, violence and clamorous discord in our world, we'd do well to reflect on the positives, life savers that sometimes go unnoticed and unheralded.

Who has been a life saver for you? Who has befriended you and pulled you up or out, when you had reached a very low point in your life? Who has delivered a message of hope and encouragement that kept you from drowning in a sea of misery or despair? ...perhaps a friend or spouse, a trusted counselor, a social worker, a priest or other man or woman of God? Or even God Himself/Herself? Would our wounded warriors who've been gifted with loving canine companions consider these pets, who are so much more than that, their life savers?

Thankfully our world has a cadre of life-saving first responders, police, firefighters, and health care workers who risk their lives for others when pandemics and other tragedies strike. We need to affirm their self-effacing courage and bravery. Often the quick thinking of lifeguards, ambulance drivers, and hotline volunteers makes a critical difference in a life hanging on by a thread. So many who have faced life-threatening injuries or illnesses are ever grateful to the skilled and dedicated doctors, nurses, and caregivers and who were their literal life savers.

Can you recall a teacher or mentor whose words of encouragement made all the difference in your life? ...or even a book which helped you turn a page in your troubled life? Passing that book on to another person in need may bring a much-needed message of hope to someone else in need. And perhaps you've discovered that pouring your energy and creativity into enjoyable pastimes can be very therapeutic, placing you onto a life-enhancing path you had never dreamed of.

We are *all* qualified to be life savers. We may never know when an act of kindness, a smile, or encouraging word will be the beacon of light touching the heart of someone in the depths of despair, making all the difference.

So I end with a question...will you be someone's life saver?

ℰᏏᏣᎡ

Book Club Questions

I Matter explored how positive events, experiences or people in your life changed our authors for the better or how they helped someone onto a better path.

- Which events come to mind before you?

- Who are your role models?

- Who has had the greatest influence on your life?

- Did any specific teacher inspire you?

- What is your fondest memory?

- Of those who are no longer in your life, whom do you miss the most? Why?

- Looking back on your life, what is your greatest accomplishment?

- What regrets do you have in life? Is there time/opportunity to fix them? How will you do so?

- What are your goals for the rest of your life?

- What do you want said of you in your eulogy? Your obituary?

- Have you done end-of-life planning?

Made in USA - Crawfordsville, IN
99869_9781735074719
10.21.2020 1453